W9-AWP-173

THE NEEDLEPOINT
COLLECTION

THE
NEEDLEPOINT
COLLECTION

SHOOTING STAR PRESS

This edition published in 1995 by

Shooting Star Press Inc.,
230 Fifth Avenue
Suite 1212
New York
NY 10001

Produced by Marshall Cavendish Books, London
(a division of Marshall Cavendish Partworks Ltd)

Copyright © Marshall Cavendish 1995
Foreword copyright © Melinda Coss 1995

All rights reserved. No part of this publication may be
reproduced, stored in a retrieval system or transmitted in any
form or by any means electronic, mechanical, photocopying,
recording or otherwise, without the prior written permission of
the publishers and the copyright holder.

ISBN 1 57335 133 4

Library of Congress Cataloging in Publication Data:
A catalog record for this book is available from
the Library of Congress

Printed and bound in Italy

Some of this material has previously appeared in
the Marshall Cavendish partwork *Discovering Needlecraft*

Contents

Foreword   6

THE PROJECTS

Contents and Introduction   7

Pillows   9

Pictures   45

For the home   59

For children   77

Charts   89

STITCHES AND TECHNIQUES

Contents and Introduction   97

Before you start   99

Finishing   103

Stitches   111

Mail-order kits   126

Index   127

Foreword

Melinda Coss

Needlepoint, sometimes known as tapestry or canvaswork, has throughout history provided stitchers with the opportunity to add a very personal touch to their homes. Nothing is more welcoming than a sofa piled with stitched throw pillows, and the vast choice of colors and canvases on the market today allows us to mix and match texture and design in a highly creative way.

Stitching, as any embroiderer will tell you, is obsessive, and needlepoint in particular, with its simple, repetitive technique, provides a comforting and therapeutic way to end a stressful day. Add to that the portability of a needlework project, the low cost of the materials, and the satisfaction of producing your own personal heirloom, and it is perhaps not so surprising that needlecraft remains one of our most popular leisure activities.

Through my years as a needlecraft designer, I have established that most stitchers share two major problems. The first is that they always underestimate their own abilities and the second is that they never have enough designs to choose from. This book should provide the solutions.

Packed with bright ideas and delicious projects, the book has something that will appeal to all tastes and levels of skill. It talks you through the stitching process from beginning to end, and what is not explained in words is there for all to see on the clearly graphed charts and beautiful photographs. It is also interspersed with hints and tips that will help you make sure that your stitched designs have a highly professional finish. In addition, it explains in detail how to turn your needlework into a decorative and useful item.

Many stitchers dread the finishing process, but often we only have to succeed at something once to realize that we are cleverer than we think. This confidence can lead on to all manner of new and satisfying accomplishments. The secret is to read the instructions carefully and to begin with a relatively simple tent stitch project, such as a greetings card. Take it step-by-step and before you know it, you will find yourself making throw pillows and framing pictures like a true expert.

Once you have mastered tent stitch, you can experiment with long stitch, which is quick to work and allows you to cover large areas of canvas in a very short time. You can also explore Bargello work and put your eye for color to the test by blending and mixing unusual combinations.

Needlecraft is not simply about following patterns and using specific materials. It is also a valuable means of self-expression. You can stitch with wool, ribbons, silk, and even strips of fabric, and you don't have to use special embroidery materials to achieve pleasing results. Try using the geometric motifs and techniques in this book to create your own individual statement. The mirror case motif, for example, could be repeated in numerous color combinations to create a panel for a pillow, while the penholder design could be stitched as a repeat border for the edge of a pillow. Experiment with different sizes of canvas mesh to make your designs bigger or smaller, and try working on a high count of mesh with stranded floss instead of wool yarn. Once you gain confidence, you will realize that your only limitation is your imagination.

On a final note, if you have children around the house, do share your skills with them. I, for one, hope to live long enough to see my grandchildren stitching, although I suspect they may be doing so on electromagnetic fibres with automatic laser-powered needle pushers. In the meantime, enjoy yourselves and this book, which will provide you with hours of inspiration.

Melinda Coss.

The Projects

Introduction 8

PILLOWS

Daffodil pillow 9

Tulip pillow 13

Bargello pillow 17

Dolphin pillow 21

Star pillow 25

Islamic pillow 29

Fan pillow 33

Fruit urn pillow 37

Vine bolster 41

PICTURES

Rose garden picture 45

Viola picture 49

Patio garden picture 51

Spring picture 55

FOR THE HOME

Geometric mirror case 59

Tissue box cover 61

Cat door-stop 65

Hall bench cushion 69

Floral rug 73

FOR CHILDREN

Shelduck pillow 77

Noah's Ark picture 81

Ginger cat picture 85

Pen holder 87

CHARTS

Dolphin pillow 89

Vine bolster 90

Star pillow 93

Spring picture 94

Tissue box cover 95

Cat door-stop 96

Introduction

Needlepoint is one of the most popular of the multitude of embroidery techniques. Because it is straightforward to work, it is simple for the beginner, but its lasting appeal has much to do with the fact that it is extremely versatile, and its beauty is undeniable.

The projects that have been collected together here provide a wide variety of items to stitch, and they are designed to appeal to beginners and needlepoint addicts alike. The clear charts are easy to follow and the finished pieces can be enjoyed for years to come by you, a member of your family, or a lucky friend. Items stitched on canvas are popular presents, and those in this book range from greeting cards that can be completed in an evening to a selection of beautiful, more intricate floral pillows and pictures.

Some of the projects, such as the pen holder, would make excellent items to sell

at charity bazaars – they can be made quickly enough that, with a little planning, you could stitch several in a variety of colors to appeal to different tastes. Perhaps one of the more complicated pieces – the cat door-stop or the beautiful bargello pillow – could be donated and sold at an auction or used as a prize in a money-spinning raffle.

There are also presents suitable for a special baby or child. The Noah's Ark picture would be a welcome addition to any child's room, and will spark off bed-time stories galore.

The more complicated projects have in them various elements that can be extracted and used individually to make small items such as greeting cards or minia-ture pictures. Some of the designs lend themselves to being stitched separately and then grouped: a tulip from the tulip pillow or one of the stars from the star pillow, for

example, could be mounted individually and hung as pictures. If you are new to needlepoint, you may want to study the various stitches detailed on pages 111–25 before you begin. Then choose your project, study the chart, pick up your needle, and start to stitch. But be warned: needlepoint can be addictive!

A NOTE ABOUT THREADS

The yarn or other threads specified in each project have been used to work the items shown in the photographs. If you are unable to purchase the materials exactly as specified, it will still be possible to work the project, but the look may be somewhat altered. Most brands of yarns and threads have similar or equivalent colors from which to choose, but the color match may not be exact.

Daffodil pillow

*Daffodils and narcissi in all shapes and sizes make this glorious bouquet
an appropriate gift for a spring birthday.*

Daffodil pillow

YOU WILL NEED

- **16 × 16in 10-gauge single canvas**
- **Paternayan Persian yarn, one skein each of:**

Pale blue 506	D391 Gray
Pearl gray 211	840 Dark red
Dark orange 831	773 Pale yellow
Old gold 750	700 Butterscotch
Dark pine green 660	613 Pale green

- **Two skeins each of:**

Dark blue 500	260 White
Orange 801	770 Golden yellow
Hunter green 610	697 Emerald green
Medium green 692	

- **Three skeins each of:**

Very pale green 654	503 Medium blue

- **Tapestry needle**
- **13 × 13in backing fabric**
- **12in square pillow form**
- **Sewing needle and thread**

colors to use. Before you begin stitching, you will need to find the center of the canvas. Fold it lightly in half each way and mark the center lines with running stitches in a brightly colored sewing thread which can be worked over and removed later if necessary. If you mark the center of the chart in pencil to correspond, it will be easier to position the stitches correctly on the canvas when you are following the chart.

Bind the raw edges of the canvas with masking tape or bias binding to stop them from fraying, and also to prevent the yarn from catching on them and snagging. This is not only annoying as you are working, but will also wear the yarn thin so that it will not cover the canvas background adequately.

You might like to organize your yarn onto a project card so that you can find each shade easily and quickly as you need it. These are available from needlecraft stores or notions departments, or you can make your own. To make your own card, simply punch holes along the edge of a strip of cardboard and loop 18–inch lengths of yarn through. Write the color number beside each one. Stretch the canvas on a scroll frame if you wish; this will keep it taut as you stitch and make it easier to keep an even tension. The canvas will also be less likely to distort in shape.

STITCHING THE PILLOW

Using two strands of Paternayan Persian yarn in the needle, begin stitching the design from the center out in half cross-stitch. To secure the end of the yarn at the beginning, leave a short end and work the first few stitches over it. When you are finishing off your length of

Daffodils and narcissi are always a beautiful and welcome sight in parks and front yards, or growing along the roadside, as they seem to symbolize the end of gray winter days with their bright petals forming glowing carpets in the spring sunshine. Part of the appeal of these lovely flowers is the huge variety in their shapes and sizes, as well as in their coloring. You may favor large, bold, and showy yellow daffodils, or you might prefer delicate little white-petaled narcissi with contrasting orange trumpets. Whatever your preference, you will enjoy stitching the gorgeous display on this needlepoint pillow. It is literally bursting out of the trellis-style frame, giving it a lively, three-dimensional quality. The finished pillow measures 12 inches square.

PREPARING TO STITCH

The color chart for the daffodil design is given opposite. Each square equals one half cross-stitch and the key indicates which yarn

KEY

Paternayan Persian yarn, as used in the Daffodil pillow:

 Pale blue – 506 (A)	Orange – 801 (F)	Dk pine green – 660 (K)	White – 260 (P)
Gray – D391 (B)	Golden yellow – 770 (G)	Hunter green – 610 (L)	Dark blue – 500 (Q)
Pearl gray – 211 (C)	Pale yellow – 773 (H)	Emerald green – 697 (M)	Medium blue – 503 (R)
Dark red – 840 (D)	Old gold – 750 (I)	Medium green – 692 (N)	Very pale green – 654 (S)
Dark orange – 831 (E)	 Butterscotch – 700 (J)	Pale green – 613 (O)	

STITCH DETAILS

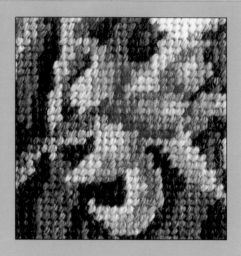

The small white daffodil has a bright trumpet in yellow, orange, and dark red. The ends of the stamens are picked out in hunter green.

The simple trellis pattern is worked in two shades of blue to contrast with the rest of the design. Work the dark blue grid first.

A variety of yellows and oranges brings the glowing narcissus to life. Dark red emphasizes the edge of the inner trumpet.

yarn, pass it under the last few stitches worked at the back. Make sure that you do not pass long strands of yarn across the back of the canvas when you are moving from one color area to another in the same color, as these can get caught up in subsequent stitching and cause a lumpy effect on the front.

Start with the gray/blue shading on the lower petal of the central daffodil; this is worked in pearl gray (211), gray (D391), and pale blue (506). Then work the rest of the petal in white (260). Complete this large daffodil by stitching the other petals in the same way, adding the trumpet in shades of yellow, orange, and dark red. The stamen is emphasized with medium green (692) and one stitch of emerald green (697).

From here, move outward to work the leaves and stems which surround this flower. These are in various shades of green, ranging from pale green (613) to dark pine green (660). The emerald green adds a bright highlight to the other, more muted, greens.

As you are working the stems and leaves, fill in each of the other flower heads as you come to them. At the top right is an all-white daffodil with gray/blue shading, and below this is another flower similar to the large central daffodil, but with a more delicate trumpet. At the bottom of the pillow are two small narcissi with pointed yellow and orange petals emphasized with dark orange (831) and dark red (840). At the top left is a classic

yellow daffodil with shading in butterscotch (700) and old gold (750), and a stamen highlighted in medium green (692). Another yellow narcissus is below this and in the bottom left-hand corner is a small white daffodil with a center in deep oranges and yellows with dark red and hunter green (610) details. At each lower corner is a bud on a slender stem.

THE BACKGROUND AND BORDER

The background to the display of daffodils is a very pale green (654), which throws the flowers into relief while blending in with the other colors. Stitch this when you have completed all the flowers, leaves, and stems, filling in carefully around all the shapes.

Finally, add the contrasting border, which is actually set behind the flowers and leaves in some places to give the impression of the daffodils bursting forth from the picture. This is worked in two shades of blue – medium blue (503) and dark blue (500) – arranged in a trellis pattern. You will find it easiest to work the dark blue parts of the trellis first and then fill in the medium blue background around it. Count the squares on the chart carefully as you do this, as the border pattern will not join up correctly if you go wrong.

FINISHING THE PILLOW

When the embroidery is complete, remove the canvas from the frame if you used one. Make sure there are no long ends of yarn left

at the back; if there are, pass them under adjacent stitches at the back and trim off short.

If necessary, restore the canvas to a square shape by blocking it as described on pages 103–4. Trim the excess canvas to ½ inch all around. Cut the backing fabric to match. With right sides facing, stitch the pillow together around three sides with backstitch, leaving the lower edge open for turning right side out. Clip across the corners, turn the pillow through to the right side, and insert the pillow form. Sew up the fourth side with slip stitch.

bright idea

Several of the daffodil or narcissi heads used in this design would make pretty motifs in their own right, particularly the ones shown as a front view. These would fill a square or slightly rectangular shape perfectly and so could be used for a pincushion, a needlecase, or a compact case. Use lengths of yarn left over from other projects, in the colors shown on the chart, adding some of the greens for part of a stem or leaves if you wish. You could either fill in a plain background in a contrasting green, or use the trellis border pattern as your background. In this case, simply extend the dark blue lines of the trellis to fill the background areas and fill with the medium blue.

Tulip pillow

Decorated with tulips in autumnal shades, this pillow band has been given the finishing touch of rich, gold piping.

Tulip pillow

The inset panel of this rich gold pillow is decorated with tulips in warm shades of rust and olive green which are offset by the gold damask fabric on each side. The overall effect is one of elegance, so this pillow would look splendid in any formal setting. Gold twisted cord on both sides of the needlepoint panel adds a touch of sparkle and highlights the golden shades in the design. The tulips are set against a rich turquoise background, which is worked in varying lengths of long stitch in a regular pattern to give a textured effect.

PREPARING THE MATERIALS

Before you start, fold your canvas in half each way to find the center and then mount it in a scroll frame. Sort and label your yarns using the key as a color reference to make following the chart quicker and easier.

The chart for the tulip panel appears on the opposite page – mark the center as your starting point. The tulip design is worked in half cross-stitch (see page 125) except for the long stitch background. Use three strands of yarn throughout.

DESIGN DETAILS

Using gold (723), start working on the central tulip. Fill in the outer petals and the stamen in the middle of the flower. Then stitch the rest of the petals in orange (801), flesh (804), and yellow (711). Add the details using rust (721).

When you have completed the first flower, move on to work the stems and leaves. Using dark green (660), fill in the stem below the completed tulip, working down the canvas. Count your stitches carefully to allow for overlapping stems in other colors. Then work

the leaves in olive (651) and lime green (693) and continue down. Add the shading on the leaves using grass green (691) and by combining colors in the needle as listed on the key opposite.

SHADED EFFECTS

When you have filled in all the green in the bottom half of the design, work the tulip in the bottom left-hand corner. Stitch the outer petals in gold, the highlights in yellow, and the center in flesh. Fill in the rust petals and add the details in brown (400) and orange.

Next move on to the larger tulip in the bottom right-hand corner. This flower is worked in rust, flesh, yellow, and orange. Add the details using brown and gold. Then work up the design in the different shades of green, filling in the stems and leaves, until all the green areas are complete.

The remaining tulip at the top of the design is worked in the same colors as the one in the bottom right-hand corner – using rust, yellow, flesh, and orange. Finally, fill in the linear details using orange and brown.

Now that all the details of the design are complete, you can move on to work the turquoise (590) background. Using three strands of yarn, work around the tulips and leaves in varying lengths of long stitch (see pages 115–6) to produce a pattern of diamond shapes. The diamond shapes are formed by working in a regular way.

First take the needle vertically over one canvas intersection to make one small long stitch. Repeat to make a second identical long stitch alongside the first. Then increase the size of the stitch to cover three holes of the

YOU WILL NEED

- **10 × 16in 12-gauge single canvas**
- **Paternayan Persian yarn (no. of skeins in brackets):**

    (2) Gold 723   721 Rust *(2)*
    (2) Orange 801   804 Flesh *(2)*
    (2) Brown 400   651 Olive *(1)*
    (1) Grass green 691   693 Lime *(1)*
    (1) Dark green 660   711 Yellow *(1)*
    (8) Turquoise 590

- **Tapestry needle**
- **⅝yd gold damask fabric**
- **⅜yd bronze damask for piping**
- **16in square pillow form**
- **32in gold twisted cord**
- **Piping cord and matching sewing thread**
- **Sewing needle**

KEY

Paternayan Persian yarn in 3 strands,
as used in the Tulip pillow:

651	723	651(2) & 691(1)
691	721	693(2) & 651(1)
693	801	651(2) & 693(1)
660	804	691(2) & 660(1)
711	400	660(2) & 691(1)

canvas, bringing the needle out one hole higher than the previous stitch and taking it vertically down to one hole below the previous stitch. Repeat to form the fourth stitch. Then work two stitches over the center canvas intersection again so that all six stitches form a diamond shape. Continue in this way until the background is finished, keeping the tension of your stitches even so that the yarn lies smooth against the canvas. Be careful not to pull the yarn too tightly or you may leave unsightly gaps between the diamond shapes.

CUTTING THE FABRIC

When you have completed all the stitching, remove the canvas from the frame and snip off any loose ends of yarn on the back. Stretch and block the canvas if necessary (see pages 103–4). Trim the canvas all around to about ½ inch from the stitched edge. This will be the seam allowance for inserting the needlepoint panel.

Then cut two pieces of gold damask fabric, each measuring 13¼ × 6¼ inches. These will form the panels on each side of the needlepoint on the front of the pillow. When you are cutting and pinning the damask, make sure that the design imprinted on the fabric will be the right way up when the panels are stitched in place. Then cut two pieces, 13¼ × 13in and 13¼ × 8½in, for the pillow backing from the same fabric – this will allow you to make a flap at the back for inserting the pillow form. Finally measure and cut two lengths of gold twisted cord 16 in long.

On the right side, pin the flat band of one length of twisted cord along one long edge of the stitched canvas, keeping the cord next to the stitching (see the steps on page 16

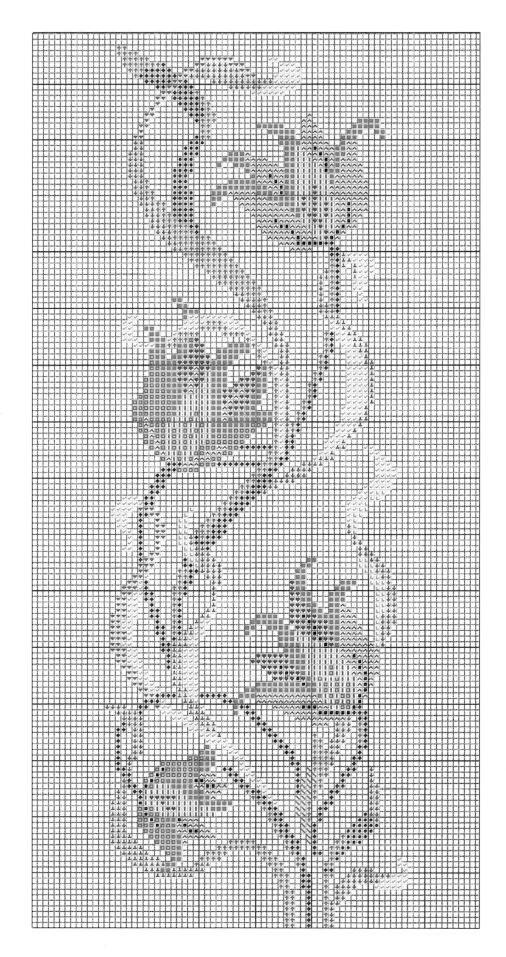

FINISHING THE PILLOW

1 Pin one length of gold twisted cord along one edge of stitched canvas on the right side. Make sure the cord abuts the stitching. Repeat on other side of stitched canvas.

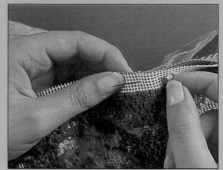

2 Place one side of stitched canvas, with cord attached, and one front damask panel right sides together. Pin damask to canvas and sew. Repeat with other damask panel.

3 Pin piping strip along edge of pillow front on the right side, matching raw edges. Take care when curving piping around corners. Trim around edges and snip into corners.

4 Turn and stitch a ½-inch hem down one side of both pieces of backing fabric. Pin to stitched canvas right sides together, the smaller piece first, then the larger one on top.

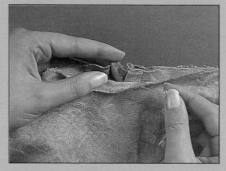

5 Where the piping strip joins at the center of the long side, overlap the two ends of the piping slightly so that they cross over to bring the ends into the seam allowance.

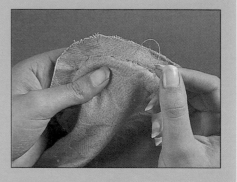

6 Baste all around the seams, remove pins, and sew in backstitch. This can be done on a sewing machine if you prefer. Make sure the stitching abuts the piping at the corners.

for details). Repeat on the other side of the canvas. Then place the canvas and one damask front panel right sides facing, lining up the seams on one side. Pin, baste, and sew in place, either by hand or machine. Stitch as close to the needlepoint as possible.

Repeat with the other front damask panel, lining it up with the other side of the canvas. Pin, baste, and sew together as before. Trim off the ends of the cord at the top and the bottom to make it a neat seam. Now that the front of your pillow is assembled with the cord running down both sides of the needlepoint panel, you are ready to make the piping.

SEAM PIPING

The piping around all four seams of the pillow is cut from the bronze-colored damask fabric in long, narrow strips (see pages 107–8 for details). Pin, baste, and sew the fabric strips together to make one long length. Wrap the fabric strip around the piping cord, right side out, and pin the edges together. Baste and sew along the length of the seam so that the piping cord is completely covered.

Pin the piping to the right side of the pillow front, matching the raw edges and taking care at the corners. Trim the ends of the piping and make sure that they meet smoothly. Baste in place, remove the pins, and sew around all four sides to secure the piping.

The two pieces of damask backing fabric are sewn to the pillow front in such a way that they overlap to make a convenient flap – follow the steps above for details on how to attach the fabric. This will allow the pillow form to be removed so that the pillow can be cleaned. Now your pillow is ready to use.

bright idea

Piping a pillow gives scope for experimenting with fabric. There is no need to feel limited in the choice of fabrics to use. Why not use a contrasting fabric to pipe around your pillow for a different look? Choose a color which complements the needlepoint design and the surrounding fabric, such as olive green, rich gold, or rust brown.

You may also want to change the overall look of the pillow by using a different color material to make it. Various shades of green, brown, or gold fabric will offset the stitched design very successfully. You might like to match your fabric with the decor in your home.

Bargello pillow

The traditional technique of bargello, or Florentine, needlepoint is used to create the wave pattern on this beautiful pillow.

Bargello pillow

YOU WILL NEED

- **18 × 18in 14-gauge single canvas**
- **Paternayan Persian yarn, three skeins each of:**
  Dark blue 510   583 Turquoise
  Pale turquoise 584   343 Lilac
  Pinkish mauve 313
- **Four skeins of:** Dark lilac 561
- **Two skeins of:** Gray 256
- **Tapestry needle**
- **16 × 16in backing fabric**
- **14in square pillow form**
- **1¾yd of twisted cord trimming**
- **Sewing needle and thread**

The beautiful patterning of bargello needlepoint is displayed to full advantage on this magnificent pillow. Although bargello work is centuries old, its timeless appearance means that it looks just as much at home in a modern setting as in a period one, and this pillow would suit a simple cane armchair as well as an old-fashioned buttonback sofa.

In spite of its intricate appearance, bargello work is not difficult to do. Once you have set up your foundation row across the canvas, the subsequent rows follow the curves exactly. The subtle marbled effect is achieved by using several different shades of just two or three main colors, graduating from dark to light. Turquoise blues, mauves, and lilacs in middle tones have been used for this pillow, and the line of the pattern is accentuated with a darker blue and a pale gray to offer some contrast. The pillow measures 14 inches square. Bargello work produces quite a firm fabric, so it is important to choose a backing fabric that matches the weight of the front of the pillow. Complete the look by adding a bright twisted cord edging.

CHOOSING COLORS

When choosing colors to work this, or any, pillow, you may find it helps if you match them to your existing decoration. If you have a spare piece of fabric or wallpaper, take it with you when you go to buy yarn. For a more subtle effect, choose shades of just one color, ranging from very dark to very light. If, however, you would like a bolder effect, choose two contrasting colors and then use at least four shades within each of their color ranges. Bargello work is shown to its best advantage when a minimum of six shades are used. Any less than this, and the subtle marbled effect will be lost.

Although wool yarn is traditionally used for bargello work, for smaller items such as glasses cases and mirror holders, you could use embroidery floss or silk. These threads give a lovely silky surface, but will require a much finer gauge of canvas.

BEFORE YOU BEGIN

Bind the raw edges of your canvas with masking tape before starting to stitch. This will prevent the yarn from catching and snagging on the rough edges. If this happens, the yarn will become thin and frayed and cause an unsightly effect on the right side of the work, especially on bargello work, in which the stitches are longer than in tent stitch. Mark the center of the canvas horizontally and vertically to help you to position the first row symmetrically. Work these lines using running stitch and sewing thread so that they can be worked over and removed when the pillow has been completed.

Mount the canvas in a scroll frame if you wish. However, if you prefer to work without a frame, you will find that bargello stitch, being vertical in structure, does not distort the canvas in the same way that tent stitch does.

STITCHING THE WAVE PATTERN

The chart for the design is given on the page opposite and shows one repeat of the wave pattern. The vertical lines show the upright stitches, each of which covers four horizontal threads of the canvas. Notice how the stitches are worked in groups of five, four, three, two,

Carefully graduated shades of blue and purple give this bargello pillow a marbled effect. Always keep shades similar to achieve this effect.

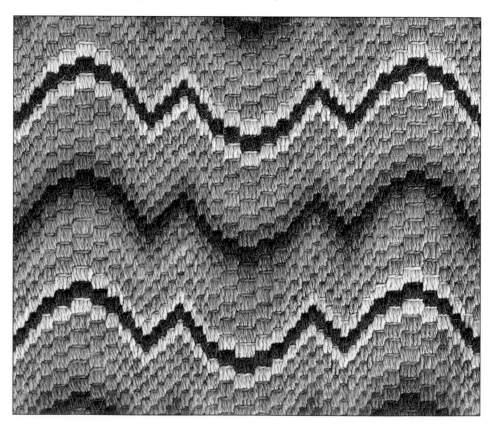

one repeat

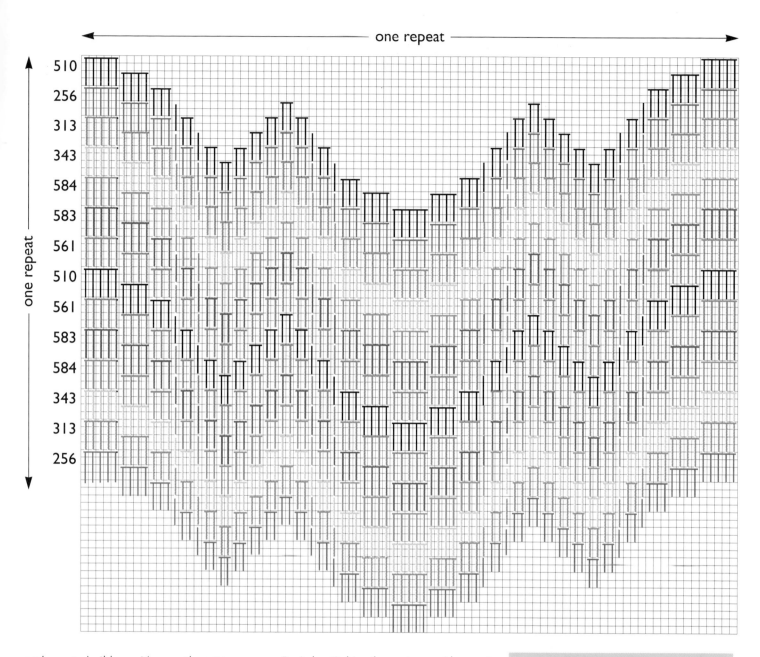

one repeat

510
256
313
343
584
583
561
510
561
583
584
343
313
256

and one to build up either gentle curves or steeply sloping lines. The different shades of color used to create the marbled effect in one pattern repeat are indicated in sequence down the left-hand side.

Two strands of Paternayan Persian yarn are used throughout for the vertical stitches. At the beginning of the first row, secure your thread end by working the first few stitches over it at the back of the canvas, and when you finish, slip the needle under the last few stitches at the back. Trim the yarn ends off neatly as you go along to prevent them from becoming tangled with subsequent stitches. This can cause a ridge on the right side of the work and may also show through stitches of another color.

Begin by stitching the center row (shown at the top of the chart) in dark blue (510) to establish the pattern. Start with the group of five stitches at the center of the pattern repeat, placing it about ¾ inch below the horizontal center line marked with basting thread. Work out from here until the first widthwise repeat is complete. Then continue out to each side of the canvas to form the first row. The other colored rows simply follow the curves of this foundation row. The next color to use is gray (256). Work the stitches over four threads of canvas, as before. Continue using each color in turn as shown on the chart above.

When you have completed one whole pattern repeat using all the colors indicated on the chart, stitch further repeats above and

be creative

The simple repeat given in the chart above could be used to make a variety of needlepoint projects.

To make a bell-pull, use the center of the chart, but alter the design on each side to create a balanced pattern. Repeat the pattern down the length of the canvas until you reach the required size.

This design could also be used to great effect in making chair covers and footstool covers. Whatever you decide to make, you may find it useful to work one repeat before you start. Measure this repeat to calculate how many you will need overall.

below until the pillow area is filled. You may find it helps to mark your pillow area with a row of running stitches. If you work these stitches following a row of holes in the canvas, you will always know where the pillow's boundaries are.

To cover the holes where different colored yarns meet, work horizontal straight stitches with one strand of Paternayan Persian yarn, as shown on the chart. This is not a common feature of bargello work, but is quite an interesting way of dividing up the blocks of color and has the added advantage of hiding any gaps that may occur between stitches on the canvas.

FINISHING THE PILLOW

Remove the canvas from the frame, if you used one. Trim any excess fabric from around the canvas, leaving a ½-inch seam allowance. Cut the backing fabric to the same size if necessary.

Place the needlepoint and the backing fabric together with right sides facing, and work backstitch or straight machine stitching around the edges of the pillow, leaving a long opening on the bottom edge for inserting the pillow form. Trim the corners and turn the pillow through to the right side. Insert the pillow form and sew up the opening with slip stitch, leaving a small opening for securing the ends of the cord. Sew on the twisted cord so that it covers the seam line. Push the ends of the cord into the opening and slipstitch to close and to hide the ends of the cord.

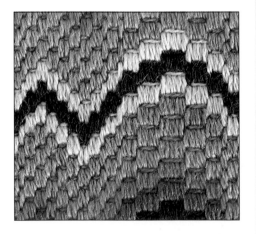

This picture shows the effect that can be created by grouping and staggering stitches. The fewer stitches there are in a group, the steeper the downward angle will be. Increase this number for a gentle curved line.

bright idea

These two illustrations show different effects that can be achieved by using varying shades of color. The top one is worked using shades of green to give a subtle pastel effect, the lower one in strong shades of bright pink and gray to create a bold, modern look. Note also the different trimming effects.

Dolphin pillow

Streamlined dolphins on this pillow leap playfully through the waves surrounded by a border depicting other endangered species.

Dolphin pillow

YOU WILL NEED

- **18 × 18in 10-gauge single canvas**
- **Paternayan Persian yarn (no. of skeins in brackets):**
  - (*1*) **Pale gray 203**   **661 Dark green** (*2*)
  - (*2*) **Charcoal 221**   **260 White** (*2*)
  - (*2*) **Cream 263**   **502 Dark blue** (*2*)
  - (*2*) **Dark gray 210**   **521 Dark jade** (*2*)
  - (*2*) **Dove gray 201**   **580 Kingfisher** (*3*)
  - (*3*) **Jade D502**   **514 Pale blue** (*4*)
  - (*6*) **Pale green 614**
- **Tapestry needle**
- **16 × 16in medium-weight backing fabric**
- **15in square pillow form**
- **Sewing needle and thread**

dangered species, the avocet and the Large Blue butterfly. It is an easy design to work in half cross-stitch, Gobelin stitch, and long stitch with some French knots.

BEFORE YOU BEGIN

The color chart for the main picture is shown opposite. Most of the design is worked in half cross-stitch, and for this each square on the chart equals one stitch. Some of the larger blocks of color in the sea are worked in Gobelin stitch over two or three canvas threads (see pages 117–8 for further details). Use the photograph as a guide here. The colors of Paternayan Persian yarn to use are shown in the key. The chart for the outer border is given in black and white on page 89. Each symbol on the chart equals one half cross-stitch and, again, the colors are given in

the key. The inner and outer borders are worked in long stitch (see pages 115–6).

Bind the raw edges of the canvas with masking tape to prevent them from fraying and to stop the yarn from catching on them as you stitch. If the yarn constantly snags on the raw canvas edges, it will quickly wear thin. Mark the horizontal and vertical center lines on the canvas with basting stitches, and mark the center lines of the chart with pencil.

WORKING THE DOLPHINS

Stretch the canvas in a frame if you wish, as it will keep its shape better if you do. To secure your thread end at the beginning of an area of stitching, leave a short length at the back of the canvas and work your first few stitches over it; to finish off neatly at the back, run the needle under the last few stitches worked.

T his beautiful design shows three dolphins leaping in unison through a turquoise sea, with white flecks of spray splashing up behind them. Because of their intelligence and friendly natures, dolphins are among the most popular animals, but their numbers are on the decline as they are constantly in danger of being caught in the vast trawl fishing nets that are now used in many places, and, being mammals, they drown when trapped underwater.

The finished pillow measures 14¼ inches square and has an outer border, which shows more dolphins as well as two other en-

This fringe shows the Paternayan yarn used in the Dolphin pillow. The colors used to work the center panel are detailed in the key on the opposite page. The additional colors are dark blue (502) – I, dark gray (210) – J, pale green (614) – K, dark green (661) – L, cream (263) – M.

Dolphins are worked both in the center panel and on the border, which also features Large Blue butterflies and avocets.

KEY

Paternayan Persian yarn,·as used in the center panel of the Dolphin pillow:

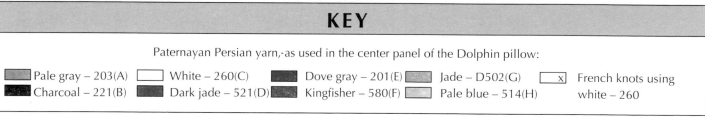

Pale gray – 203(A) White – 260(C) Dove gray – 201(E) Jade – D502(G) French knots using
Charcoal – 221(B) Dark jade – 521(D) Kingfisher – 580(F) Pale blue – 514(H) white – 260

23

Using all three strands of the yarn in the needle throughout, start stitching with the center dolphin. Fill in the body in dove gray (201) with charcoal (221) fins and body stripe, and details in pale gray (203) and white (260). Work the other two dolphins in the same way.

When the dolphins are complete, fill in the sea behind them. Use either half cross-stitch or Gobelin stitch, using the photograph as a color guide. The sea is worked in pale blue (514), kingfisher (580), jade (D502), and dark jade (521). The spray is stitched in white (260), and the flecks of foam are worked in French knots (see page 125) using the white yarn again to make them stand out from the background.

When the central panel is complete, stitch the outer border following the chart on page 89. Work the dark green inner edge first in long stitch over two canvas threads. Make vertical stitches at the top and bottom, and horizontal stitches at

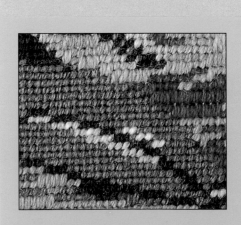

An endangered avocet is worked at each of the four corners of the border.

bright idea

If you wish, this design could also be used to make a stunning square picture to give to a friend who is a conservationist or an animal lover. The stitched border with butterflies, dolphins and avocets means that you do not need a mount. The completed needlepoint can simply be mounted on a backing board and set straight into a frame.

the sides. At the corners, slant the stitches toward the center panel in order to create a mitered effect.

Next work the avocets, the dolphins, and the Large Blue butterflies inside the border. The butterflies' bodies can be worked in long stitch if you wish. Now fill in the background in pale green (614) and complete the border by adding the outer edge in dark green long stitch.

FINISHING THE PILLOW

If necessary, block the needlepoint (see pages 103–4). Trim the excess canvas to leave a seam allowance of ½in. Cut the backing fabric to match. With right sides facing, pin the backing fabric to the needlepoint. Using backstitch, sew around the edge of the pillow, leaving an opening on the fourth side. Clip the corners and turn through to the right side. Insert the pillow form through the opening and slipstitch to close.

STITCH DETAILS

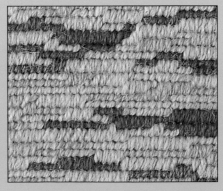

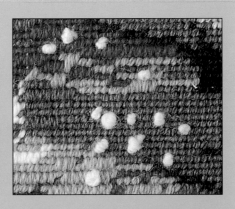

The dolphins are worked entirely in half cross-stitch in shades of gray and white to give them a smooth, sleek outline.

The ripples on the sea are given texture by using Gobelin stitch as well as half cross-stitch in shades of blue and green.

White French knots are used to make the flecks of foam flying up from the sea, so that they stand out from the picture.

Star pillow

Bold colors and a strong geometric design combine to give this needlepoint pillow instant impact.

Star pillow

YOU WILL NEED

- **16 × 16in 12-gauge single canvas**
- **Paternayan Persian yarn, one skein each of:**
  - Coral 873   860 Copper
  - Brown 920   563 Sky blue
- **Two skeins each of:**
  - Navy 571   550 Royal blue
  - Purple 311   661 Pine green
  - Grass green 630   651 Olive green
  - Aqua 523
- **Three skeins of:** Pale coral 805
- **Tapestry needle**
- **14½ × 14½in backing fabric**
- **12-in square pillow form**
- **Matching sewing thread**

Evocative of eastern tiles, this deceptively intricate-looking design is made up of a simple star motif that is repeated in nine different color combinations and set on a multicolored checked background. A single pillow, or more, with such a dazzling effect would be the perfect complement for traditional oriental rugs, ikat, and other ethnic-style furnishings.

The pillow measures 12 inches square and is embroidered in four simple needlepoint stitches – tent stitch, brick stitch, long-legged cross-stitch, and long stitch. The finished pillow has a contrast backing fabric and a simple hand-sewn closure.

PREPARING THE CANVAS

To help you center your design, first mark the center of the canvas both horizontally and vertically with a row of basting stitches. Mark the corresponding lines on the chart in pencil. You may also find it helpful to mark every tenth hole on the canvas to match the thicker lines on the chart.

Bind the raw edges of the canvas with masking tape or bias binding to prevent them from fraying and to stop the yarn from catching on the threads. If this happens, the yarn can become thin and will then not cover the canvas properly. Stretch your canvas in a scroll frame – this helps to keep the canvas even while being stitched and leaves both hands free to work with one below and the other on top of your embroidery.

STITCHING THE DESIGN

The design is worked using two strands of yarn in the needle throughout. Following the color chart on the opposite page, begin the design centrally by filling in the long stitch blocks that make up the center of the star motif (see pages 115–6 for how to work long stitch). Refer to page 92 for a detailed diagram of one corner of the pillow showing how the stitches are positioned on the canvas mesh. Notice that some stitches, such as the blocks of long stitches in the middle of the stars, have additional stitches placed at the top and bottom of each block to cover the canvas

mesh completely. Fill in the star and its outline using tent stitch (see pages 111–2, Continental tent stitch, for how to work these areas of the design).

Continuing out from the center, fill in the background around the star motif with brick stitch (see pages 119–20). The brick stitches

are worked over two of the canvas threads and in order to work neatly up to a straight edge, around the stars, and the outer border, for example, it is important to work half

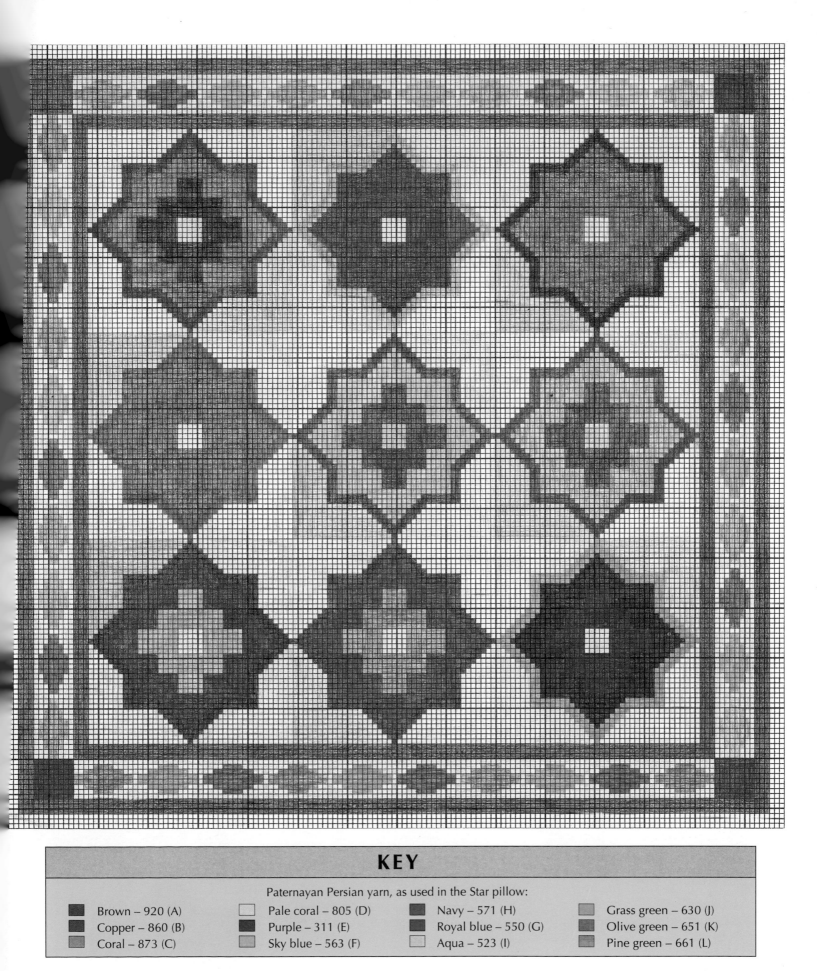

KEY

Paternayan Persian yarn, as used in the Star pillow:

Brown – 920 (A)
Copper – 860 (B)
Coral – 873 (C)

Pale coral – 805 (D)
Purple – 311 (E)
Sky blue – 563 (F)

Navy – 571 (H)
Royal blue – 550 (G)
Aqua – 523 (I)

Grass green – 630 (J)
Olive green – 651 (K)
Pine green – 661 (L)

STITCH DETAILS

Extra long stitches are worked to prevent any canvas from showing through around the blocks that make up the star motifs.

The outer border is worked in a combination of long stitch and tent stitch to create a raised, textured effect.

Brick stitch is a quick and easy way to fill in the background of the star motifs; each stitch is worked over two canvas threads.

stitches, over just one canvas thread, to fill the space. Complete all the stars and the background in the same way as detailed for the center square.

Using long-legged cross-stitch (see pages 121–2) and navy (571), work the inner and outer borders around the pillow. Start at one corner and work the borders around the pillow, turning the work as you go to achieve a continuous stitching line. Then, using long stitch worked in sequence over several blocks of threads, embroider the diamond border design using three shades of green. Fill in around these shapes with tent stitch, using very pale coral (805), working two stitches between each block, as shown on the chart. Add the four corners using royal blue (550) and working long stitch diagonally to cover four blocks on the canvas. If you wish, these can be worked using long stitch vertically or horizontally – the effect will be the same.

FINISHING THE PILLOW

Remove the needlepoint from the frame and block, if necessary, following the instructions on pages 103–4. Trim the excess canvas from around the design, leaving a 1/2-inch seam allowance all around.

Cut the backing fabric to the same size as the trimmed canvas, and with right sides facing, pin and baste the two pieces together around the edges. With the needlepoint uppermost, machine stitch or backstitch, working the stitches close to the needlepoint to prevent the canvas from showing through the seam. Leave a 9-inch opening in the bottom edge.

Snip across the corners to reduce the bulk in these areas and turn the pillow through to the right side. Lightly press the backing fabric. Insert the pillow form and with matching sewing thread, slip stitch the opening to close.

If you wish, you can now add a satin twisted cord to the outer edges of the completed pillow. You will need to buy 1 1/2 yards of cord, taking care to match the weight to that of the finished pillow. When you are finishing the pillow, leave a small opening in the center of the lower edge for securing the raw ends of the cord. Slip stitch the cord around the outer edges of the pillow to cover the seam. Insert the raw ends into the small opening to hide them and slip stitch the opening to close.

be creative

This design is ideal for using up any odd skeins of Paternayan Persian yarn that you may have left over from other projects. You could work each star shape and four background sections in different colors, perhaps using co-ordinating colors for each one. This will give the finished design a patchworked look and create a more country feel.

Alternatively, simplify the design by working all the stars using the same color combinations and the four background sections using the same color for all of them.

Each star motif is worked using a different combination of the six strong colors, but has a lighter colored center. The first star below uses navy (571) and pine green (661) for the star and very pale coral (805) for the center.

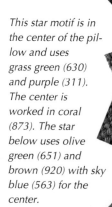

This star motif is in the center of the pillow and uses grass green (630) and purple (311). The center is worked in coral (873). The star below uses olive green (651) and brown (920) with sky blue (563) for the center.

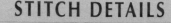

Islamic pillow

*The pattern of this richly colored needlepoint pillow is based on
the geometric designs found on oriental rugs.*

Islamic pillow

The patterns of oriental rugs are endlessly fascinating with their interlocking geometric shapes and interesting small motifs and medallions. Much of the appeal of these rugs and carpets lies in their rich and subtle coloring, often faded into beautiful soft hues by age and wear.

This pillow is adapted from a typical Persian rug design with a large central motif and a background further embellished with scattered smaller shapes. Borders are very important in oriental rug designs, often incorporating many bands of intricate patterning. The border of this pillow echoes the medium blue shade of the central motif and is finished at each corner with a diamond shape. The finished pillow measures 13½ × 14¼ inches.

PREPARING THE CANVAS

Before you begin stitching, bind the raw edges of the canvas with masking tape to stop the yarn from catching on it and snagging as you work. Mark the center lines horizontally and vertically with lines of basting stitches to help you position the pattern correctly. Mount the canvas in a scroll frame to keep it taut as you stitch and so prevent it from distorting.

STITCHING THE DESIGN

A color chart for the Islamic design is shown opposite – note that the pattern is not symmetrical. Each square on the chart represents one half cross-stitch. The key shows you which colors to use. Complete each area of color before beginning the next and avoid taking long strands across the back of the work. Secure your yarn when you begin stitching by working the first few stitches over it, and finish it by slipping the needle under the last few stitches at the back. Do not run a dark-colored yarn under light-colored stitches as it may show through at the front of the work.

With two strands of yarn in the needle, begin stitching centrally with the small diamond in burnt orange (830), navy (570), and fawn (465). Still working from the center outward, work the inner medallion in fawn with patterning and outlines in dark green (D516), medium green (D522), khaki (453), and burnt orange. Then work the outer medallion in

medium blue (544) with a fawn and khaki outline and the small patterned shapes in various shades.

The background is worked in burnt orange with small motifs of different shapes scattered over it. Outline this area with lines of fawn and navy (570). The outer area is worked in navy, again with scattered small motifs. Add the border in medium blue with lozenge shapes in dark green and burnt orange, surrounded by lines of navy and burnt orange. Finally, outline the fawn and medium blue medallions in dark brown (420) backstitch. When the needlepoint is complete, take it off the frame. If it needs stretching back into shape, block it as shown page 103–4.

FINISHING THE PILLOW

Trim any excess canvas from around the edge of the design, leaving a ½in seam allowance. Cut the backing fabric to match. Using the bias binding and the piping cord, make a length of covered piping to fit around the edges of the pillow (see page 107–8). Pin and baste in place around the needlepoint close to the stitched edge, matching the raw edges and placing the ends of the covered piping in the center of the lower edge. Machine or backstitch to secure. Baste the backing fabric in place over the needlepoint, enclosing the covered piping. Machine or backstitch around three sides, leaving the bottom edge open. Insert the pillow form and slip stitch to close, enclosing the ends of the piping in the seam.

YOU WILL NEED

- **18 × 18in 10-gauge single canvas**
- **Paternayan Persian yarn (no. of skeins in brackets):**

(?) **Burnt orange 830   570 Navy (?)**
(?) **Medium blue 544   D522 Med. green (?)**
(?) **Dark green D516   420 Dark brown (?)**
(?) **Khaki 453   465 Fawn (?)**

- **Tapestry needle**
- **16 × 16in backing fabric**
- **14in square pillow form**
- **1¾yd medium piping cord**
- **1¾yd matching bias binding**
- **Sewing needle and thread**

KEY

Paternayan Persian yarn, as used in the Islamic pillow:

Burnt orange – 830 (A)

Navy – 570 (B)

Medium blue – 544 (C)

Medium green – D522 (D)

Dark green – D516 (E)

Dark brown – 420 (F) – backstitching

Khaki – 453 (G)

Fawn – 465 (H)

COLOR COMBO A

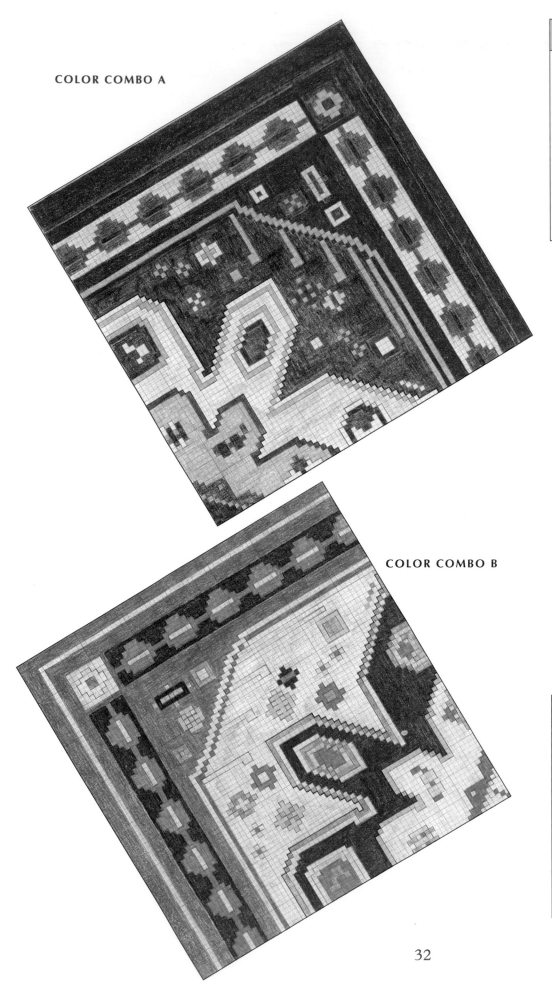

COLOR COMBO B

KEY

Paternayan Persian yarn,
as used in color combo A:

- Use Brown (420) for Burnt orange (830)
- Use Dark red (900) for Navy (570)
- Use Mink (406) for Medium blue (544)
- Use Bottle (520) for Med. green (D522)
- Use Rose (911) for Dark green (D516)
- Use Yellow (712) for Khaki (453)
- Use Gold (701) for Fawn (465)
- Use Black for Dark brown (420)

CREATE YOUR OWN LOOK

There are a number of traditional oriental color combinations that could be used to make a set of pillows. When you are changing colors within a design, it is important to replace a light color with another light one and a dark color with another dark color; otherwise, the design may lose its impact and balance. Finding a source of inspiration, such as a piece of pottery or a mosaic pattern with colors in it that you would like to use, can help with planning the design.

Here we have shown two variations you might like to use. The charts show one quarter of the pillow and the keys given above and below show the Paternayan Persian colors that replace those given on the main chart on page 31. To work either of these color combos, follow the main chart, but change the colors to those shown on the new key.

To design a color combination of your own, copy the outline of the design onto graph paper, then choose your colors to replace the original ones. Following the chart, color in one corner to check that the new color scheme works successfully.

KEY

Paternayan Persian yarn,
as used in color combo B:

- Use Beige (475) for Burnt orange (830)
- Use Bright blue (580) for Navy (570)
- Use Plum (910) for Medium blue (544)
- Use Yellow (712) for Med. green (D522)
- Use Dark green (D516) as on main chart
- Use Gold (732) for Khaki (453)
- Use Pale blue (523) for Fawn (465)
- Use Black for Dark brown (420)

Fan pillow

*The beautiful design on this pillow is made up of two overlapping fans
decorated with bright-colored flowers.*

Fan pillow

YOU WILL NEED

- **14 × 16in 12-gauge single canvas**
- **Paternayan Persian yarn, one skein each of:**

Gold 700	423 Medium brown
Red 950	942 Bright pink
Medium pink 904	914 Pale pink
Plum 900	661 Dark green
Olive green 950	502 Airforce blue
Leaf green 621	630 Bright green
Pale blue 564	561 Medium blue

- **Two skeins each of:**

Cream 261	727 Pale yellow
Medium yellow 702	594 Med. turquoise
Pale turquoise 595	443 Tan
Dark brown 441	

- **Tapestry needle**
- **14¼ × 14¼in backing fabric**
- **11 × 12½in pillow form**
- **Sewing needle and thread**

The vibrant colors in this fan pillow make it an eye-catching accessory for a living room or bedroom. Although the pattern looks quite complex, it is not difficult to stitch as it is worked throughout in half cross-stitch. The finished pillow measures 11 × 12½ inches.

BEFORE YOU BEGIN

Bind the raw edges of the canvas with masking tape before you begin stitching; otherwise, the yarn can easily snag on the canvas threads. Mark the center of the canvas both horizontally and vertically with lines of basting stitches. Mount the canvas in a scroll frame to keep it taut during stitching. This will prevent the canvas from being pulled out of shape by the stitches.

STARTING TO STITCH

The chart for the fan design is shown opposite. Each square on the chart represents one half cross-stitch. The key below shows you which colors to use. Work in half cross-stitch throughout, using two strands of yarn in the needle. To secure the yarn end at the back of the work, work the first few stitches over it; to finish it neatly, slip the needle under the last few stitches at the back.

Begin stitching centrally with the stem and small leaves trailing from the yellow flower on the blue fan. Complete this stem with the small pink flower and the cluster of leaves at the end. Next work the yellow flower and add the leaves and the other trailing stem which form part of this flower, finishing with the blue segmented flower with a dark pink center. Stitch the other floral motifs on the blue fan and fill in the striped background using the turquoise yarns. Stitch the struts in brown and cream.

Now work the large rose on the yellow fan. Add its leaves and stem, then work the rose bud with its leaves and stem. Fill in the striped background of the fan with the two yellows. Work the struts as for the blue fan. Finish the design by working the rest of the cream background around the fans.

FINISHING OFF

Block the canvas if necessary (see pages 101–2). Trim the canvas edges to ½ inch and trim the backing fabric to match. Pin the backing fabric to the needlepoint, right sides facing, and sew together with backstitch, leaving an opening for inserting the pillow form. Clip the corners and turn through to the right side. Insert the pillow form. (If you wish to make your own pillow form, see pages 105–6.) Sew up the opening with slipstitch. For a decorative finish, slip stitch a contrasting twisted satin cord around the edges of the pillow to cover the seam lines. Tuck the ends into the seam at the lower edge.

KEY

Paternayan Persian yarn, as used in the Fan pillow:

☐	261		700
■	443		564
■	441		561
■	423	⊠	502
☐	914		621
	904		630
■	942	■	661
■	950		650
■	900		594
☐	727	☐	595
	702		

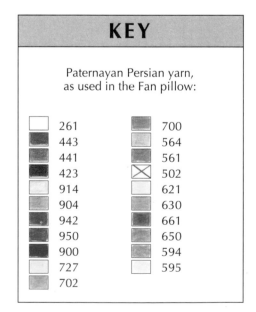

bright idea

In addition to making an attractive pillow, the fan design with its bold, graphic lines would work well as a picture. Turn the raw canvas edges back over a piece of acid-free cardboard and lace from side to side and from top to bottom, using a strong thread.

The needlepoint can be mounted and framed as you wish. You could choose a bright color for the frame which picks out one of the shades in the fans, like the blue shown here. In this case, it is best to use a mat of a muted color. Alternatively, for a more exotic effect, try a frame with a gilded or a lacquered look and a mat of a stronger color.

A more ambitious needleworker could make a stunning picture by working one of the fan motifs only and mounting it shaped as a single fan. Follow the instructions for embroidering the blue fan without working any background around it.

Cut out a piece of cardboard to the exact size of the fan and mount the embroidery over it, snipping into the points where the struts meet and gluing these edges to the back of the board. Snip into the curved outer edge and turn the canvas over the cardboard. Use dabs of glue and lacing to secure the work. Mount in an upright position on a contrasting background.

STITCH DETAILS

Begin by stitching the trailing stems and the leaves of the yellow flower on the turquoise fan.

When you have finished working the brown struts, fill in the cream areas of background between them.

The shading on the large rose on the yellow fan is achieved with several graduated shades of pink.

Fruit urn pillow

Embroider this stunning design in half cross-stitch and then add
a satin cord edging to make an elegant pillow.

Fruit urn pillow

YOU WILL NEED

- **16 × 16in 10-gauge single canvas**
- **Paternayan Persian yarn, five skeins of: Rust 870**
- **Three skeins each of:**
    - Mink 872   410 Brown
    - Gold 731   645 Greenish beige
    - Bottle green 640
- **Two skeins each of:**
    - Wine 940   903 Bright pink
    - Purple 310   853 Orange
    - Olive green 643   695 Pale green
    - Medium green 653
- **One skein each of:**
    - Pale pink 326   312 Mauve
    - Red 970   651 Leaf green
- **Tapestry needle**
- **16 × 16in backing fabric**
- **12 × 15in pillow form**
- **1½yd of satin cord**
- **Sewing needle and thread**

scroll frame to keep the tension even during stitching. Start each area of color by leaving a long end of yarn on the wrong side of the canvas which can be worked over by the first few stitches. End by slipping the needle back through the last few stitches to secure the thread.

STITCHING THE DESIGN

Work the design in half cross-stitch using two strands of yarn throughout. Half cross-stitch does not distort the canvas as much as continental tent stitch, although it does not give such a dense, well-covered fabric. It also uses less yarn, but care must be taken to ensure that thin ends of yarn are not used as the canvas may then show through the thinly stitched yarn.

Using the chart opposite as a guide to the colors to use, start at the center marked point by stitching the first leaf. Always finish one

KEY

Paternayan Persian yarn, as used in the Fruit urn pillow:

653 (A)		940 (J)	
695 (B)		903 (K)	
645 (C)		326 (L)	
970 (D)		312 (M)	
853 (E)		310 (N)	
731 (F)		640 (O)	
872 (G)		651 (P)	
870 (H)		643 (Q)	
410 (I)			

You may find it useful to fasten a sample of each color onto a piece of cardboard, as we have here, for easy reference as you stitch. Write the color numbers as given on the skein band next to each sample to jog your memory.

Based on a garden scene featuring a classic Greek urn surrounded with fruit and flowers, this needlepoint pillow will look beautiful in a traditional or modern setting. With a finished size of 12 × 15 inches, this design makes a small chair cushion. The design is worked in half cross-stitch in rich shades of greens, browns, pinks, purples, and reds. Complete the pillow by adding a coordinated satin cord edging and a contrasting fabric backing.

BEFORE YOU START

Find the center of your canvas by folding it in half each way. Mark the center lines with lines of basting stitches worked with sewing thread. To help you read the chart, you might also like to make lines of basting every 10 or 20 threads. These can be stitched over and removed when the design is complete. Use a bright color that will be easily seen as you work. Mark the center of the chart in pencil.

Now bind the edges of the canvas with masking tape or bias binding to prevent them from fraying and then mount the canvas in a

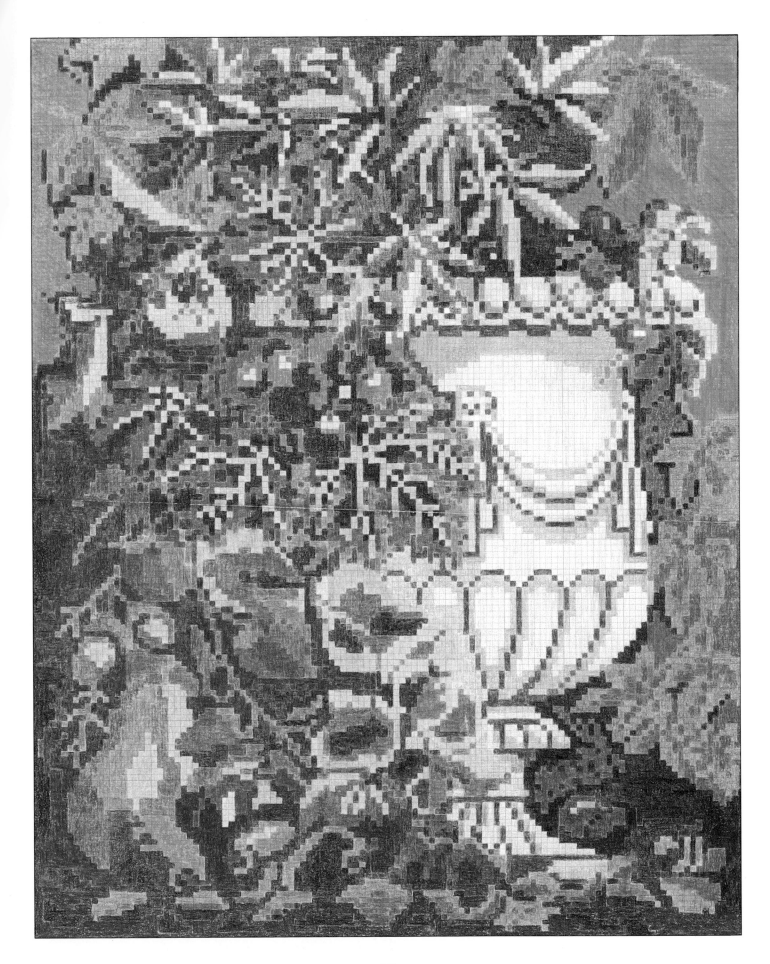

area of color before starting another, and try not to pass yarn across the back of the work as these strands may become caught up in subsequent stitches and create an unsightly effect on the right side of the work. Passed yarn also makes areas effectively a double thickness, producing an undesirable ridged effect on the front and preventing the design from lying flat when completed. Continuing out from the center point, complete the design.

FINISHING THE PILLOW

If the canvas has become misshapen during stitching, block your design (see pages 103–4), and then trim excess fabric from around the finished design, leaving a ½in seam allowance. Cut the backing fabric to the same size, making sure the edges are square.

When choosing a backing fabric, try to find one that matches the weight of the finished work to give the pillow some substance. Firmly woven furnishing and upholstery fabrics are usually best. Too light a fabric will cause the pillow to sag.

With right sides of the backing piece and the finished design facing, use a small backstitch, or machine stitch, close to the edge of the embroidered stitches to join the two pieces together, leaving the bottom edge open. Trim the corners diagonally to reduce the bulk and turn the pillow cover through to the right side. Insert the pillow form and slip stitch the opening to close, leaving ¾in open at the center of the seam to hide the ends of the twisted satin cord. Slip stitch the satin cord in position around the edges of the pillow to cover the seam, starting and ending at center of the bottom edge. Push raw ends of the cord into the opening to hide them and slip stitch the remaining opening to close.

HELPFUL

You may find it useful to work all the small areas of color or single stitches first and then build up the design around them. In this case, the best way to secure the ends is to take the needle through from the right side to the wrong side about ¾ inches from where the first stitch is to start. Leave a long end on the right side and work over the passed thread on the wrong side with subsequent stitches. The long ends on the right side can then be trimmed when secure. This can also be useful if you need to find an end for unpicking.

HINTS

bright idea

The rectangular shape of this design makes it perfect to use as a picture. First block the design, but do not trim away the excess canvas. Now mount it on a piece of heavy cardboard, folding extra canvas to the wrong side and securing it with masking tape and lacing. Complete with a contrasting mat and a plain wooden frame.

Vine bolster

*This needlepoint bolster, worked in simple half cross-stitch, is decorated
with succulent grapes in rich and splendid colors.*

Vine bolster

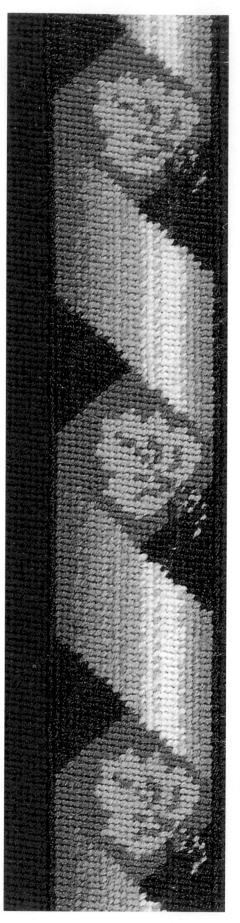

E choing the opulence and splendor of ancient Rome, this bolster would look rich and elegant in any formal setting. The grape vine, heavy with ripened fruit, twists its way around the bolster shape adding to the movement in the design. The overall shape of the bolster is fluid and free-flowing like the rich red wine produced in abundance from the grapes themselves.

Easy to work, the bolster is stitched in half cross-stitch, but the finished result looks very impressive. The completed vine needlepoint is made up into a bolster using rich green velvet and gold cord edging which add to the overall luxurious effect.

PREPARING YOUR MATERIALS

Use the illustrations left and opposite as a visual reference to working the bolster border and grape design. The symbol chart for the whole design is given on pages 90–2. Refer to the key as a guide to symbols and colors. The design is worked in two strands of Paternayan Persian yarn throughout.

It is a good idea to identify your yarns and label them before you start to stitch for easy color reference later. You might like to make a swatch card like the one pictured below to help you when choosing your colors. This

also prevents unnecessary mistakes when you are threading your needle with a new color.

Before you start to stitch, find the center of your canvas by folding it in half each way. Then mark the center point of the design on the symbol chart. This will be your starting point – it will help you to keep the design centered on the canvas. Then mount the canvas on a scroll frame to prevent distortion. As

YOU WILL NEED

- **20 × 27½ in 14-gauge single canvas**
- **Paternayan Persian yarn (no. of skeins in brackets):**
  - (*3*) Honey 732   312 Violet (*3*)
  - (*3*) Yellow 726   731 Coffee (*4*)
  - (*4*) Pale green 694   423 Brown (*2*)
  - (*2*) Lavender 314   600 Dark green (*9*)
  - (*7*) Grass green 692   310 Grape (*10*)
  - (*24*) Cream 263
- **Tapestry needle**
- **20 × 27½ in green velvet fabric**
- **1⅜ yd gold twisted cord**
- **18in-long bolster pad, 7 inches in circumference**
- **Sewing needle and thread**

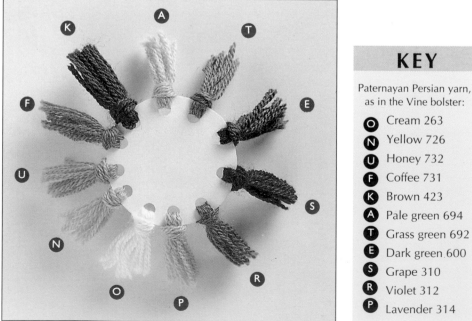

KEY

Paternayan Persian yarn, as in the Vine bolster:

- (O) Cream 263
- (N) Yellow 726
- (U) Honey 732
- (F) Coffee 731
- (K) Brown 423
- (A) Pale green 694
- (T) Grass green 692
- (E) Dark green 600
- (S) Grape 310
- (R) Violet 312
- (P) Lavender 314

WORKING THE DESIGN

For a smoother finish, separate the strands of yarn and then recombine the appropriate number of strands in your needle. This helps the yarn to lie flat against the canvas. In this case, you will need to separate the three-stranded Paterna-yan yarn and put two strands back together.

Start in the center of the design by threading your needle with two strands of violet (312) and filling in your first bunch of grapes. Work half cross-stitch in rows wherever possible for a smoother finish; it is easier to keep the tension of your stitches even when you are working in rows. Then add the shading to the grapes using grape (310), using the symbol chart as a guide. The highlights on the grapes are worked in lavender (314). This use of different shades of color will produce a three-dimensional effect and add depth to the design.

When you have completed your first bunch of grapes, work the vine leaves. Stitch the main color in the leaves, first using grass green (692). Then add the outlines of the leaves in dark green (600), working around the uneven shapes. This will add some definition to the design. Then work the light areas on the leaves in pale green (694).

Refer to the key often when working in shades which are very similar. If you have labeled your yarns in advance, you will be able to work the shades of brown on the stems without any problem. Continue to work the grapes and the leaves, following the symbol chart, until the design details are complete. Next you can stitch the gold ribbon border design which runs down both edges of the canvas.

RIBBON BORDER

When you have finished all the grape and vine details, you are ready to stitch the ribbon border using the different shades of gold. Use the key provided on page 42 when you are selecting your yarns since the blended shades of gold in the ribbon look very similar. The highlights are filled in using cream. When you have finished working the gold ribbon itself, add the small green vine leaves in pale green and work their shading in dark green. Then fill in the background of the ribbon using dark green yarn (600) and stitch the surrounding border in grape (310). Once one border is complete, repeat the gold ribbon design down the other side of the canvas, counting the stitches carefully.

PROFESSIONAL RESULTS

When you have worked all the design details, the last step is to fill in the cream background.

a general stitching rule, work all the grape and leaf details of the vine design first, then work the outer ribbon borders and then the cream background.

The symbol chart for the bolster design appears on pages 90–2. Use the illustrations above and below as a visual reference to how the colors work together, bringing the design to life. Shading on the grapes and leaves produces a three-dimensional effect.

43

Remember to work to an even tension and do not work with a length of yarn which is more than 18 inches; otherwise, it may snag and look messy. To achieve a smooth result, let the needle fall from your hand every so often to allow the yarn to unwind. This is particularly important when working large areas in light colors as an uneven tension will show in the finished needlepoint.

FINISHING TOUCHES

Once all the stitching is complete, remove the canvas from the frame and snip off any loose thread ends at the back. Hold the finished needlepoint up to the light to check for any missed stitches and add these if necessary.

Before making your bolster, you will need to block and reshape your canvas (see pages 103–4). Finally, see the steps below for details on how to make the bolster.

FINISHING THE BOLSTER

1 Mark a round template for the round ends of the bolster from stiff cardboard. The template should measure 4½ inches in radius. Draw a second inner circle on the card measuring 3½ inches in radius.

2 Fold velvet right sides together, pin the template, and cut out the fabric circles. Cut the outer circle from the template, center small circle on the back of each piece of fabric, and use it to mark the seam allowance.

3 Pin the gold braid to one end of the stitched design so that the piping abuts the edge of the needlepoint closely as above. Baste and sew in place. Repeat with the other end.

4 Snip unstitched canvas edges. Pin long sides of canvas at each end to make a tube. Mark velvet circles in halves on seam allowance and match them to the canvas seam and the center of the needlepoint edge.

5 Fit one velvet circle to the edge of the needlepoint stitching, keeping the braid inside the work and the seam abutting the edge of the braid very closely. Repeat on the other end.

6 Turn the pillow right side out and insert the bolster pad. Turn in the unstitched canvas edges and pin together. Slipstitch down the length of the bolster using thread to match the background yarn.

Rose garden picture

This charming picture shows a rose-strewn path
leading down to a secluded bench.

Rose garden picture

YOU WILL NEED

- **12 × 14in 14-gauge single canvas**
- **Paternayan Persian yarn, one skein each of:**

Fawn 405	946 Pale pink
Taupe 485	261 Cream
Charcoal 221	452 Brown
Purple 331	333 Lilac
Lavender 323	910 Rose pink
Pale fuchsia 354	904 Medium pink
Salmon 843	772 Yellow
Bright green 693	622 Pale green
Sage green 604	671 Lime green
Spring green 634	D516 Dark green
Leaf green 612	

- **Two skeins of:**

  Sky blue 594
- **Tapestry needle**

Bind the edges of the canvas with masking tape to prevent the yarn from catching on them as you stitch. Mount the prepared canvas in a scroll frame; this will keep the canvas taut during stitching. This will mean that your stitches are all worked to the same tension, since using a frame allows you to work with both hands free so that you can stitch more quickly, with one hand on top of the canvas and one hand below.

STITCHING THE DESIGN

Following the chart on the opposite page and the key on this page, begin to work the rose garden design starting at the center point of the canvas and the chart. Use two strands of yarn in the needle and half cross-stitch

This swatch card shows the shades of yarn used to work the Rose garden picture. The key above shows the colors on the chart that correspond to the yarn numbers.

KEY

Paternayan Persian yarn, as used in the Rose garden picture:

	405 (A)		904 (L)
	946 (B)		843 (M)
	485 (C)		772 (N)
●	261 (D)		693 (O)
	221 (E)		622 (P)
	452 (F)		604 (Q)
	331 (G)		671 (R)
	333 (H)		634 (S)
	323 (I)		D516 (T)
	910 (J)		612 (U)
	354 (K)		594 (V)

Rose-covered arches lead the viewer's eye down a grassy path to a white bench at the end of the garden. Standard rose bushes are combined with flower borders and a brick wall to complete the picture. The design is worked in a variety of garden-fresh pinks, purples, and greens.

Worked on 14-mesh canvas using two strands of Paternayan Persian yarn, the finished design measures 7¼ x 9½ inches and is easy to work in half cross-stitch.

BEFORE YOU START

The chart for the design is given on the following page; the key above right shows which shades of Paternayan Persian yarn to use. To help you to follow the chart, mark the horizontal and vertical centers on the canvas with lines of basting stitches and mark the center of the chart in pencil.

Keep track of the 22 colors needed to work the design by attaching lengths of yarn to a swatch card and marking them with the skein color number. Swatch cards are available from craft stores, or you can make your own by punching a row of holes along one side of a piece of cardboard.

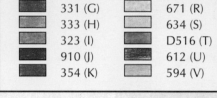

throughout. Cut lengths of yarn no longer than 18in, so that they do not wear thin as you stitch. Where possible, finish one area of color before starting another and avoid carrying yarn across the back of the work from one area to another. This can make the work very bulky and prevent it from sitting smoothly when framed. Do not start stitching with a knot, but leave a long end on the wrong side of the work. Holding this down, carefully work your first few stitches over it. End an area of stitching by threading the needle back through the last few stitches worked. Always trim off any loose ends as you work to keep them from becoming caught up with subsequent stitching.

As the picture builds up, you may find it helpful to have several needles threaded with the colors in use. Those not actually being used can be pinned in the margin of the canvas until they are needed again. Take care to keep these yarns well away from those you are using so that you do not work over them accidentally.

The rose arches are covered with climbing roses, worked in a variety of bright pinks and purples with vivid green leaves and stems.

─── **HANDY** ───

To help you to keep your place when you are following the chart, use a see-through plastic ruler to mark each part of the chart as you work it. This way you will be able to see the row you are working and the row below it. When you put your work down, use a small piece of masking tape to mark your position on the chart.

You may also find it helpful to use a line of basting to mark every tenth hole along the side edges of the canvas to correspond to the heavier black lines on the chart; you will have a handy reference as you stitch and be less likely to make mistakes.

─── **HINT** ───

FINISHING OFF

When you have completed stitching the design, remove the canvas from the frame and block it if necessary to return it to its original shape (see pages 103–4). Mount the canvas on a piece of acid-free mounting board, by folding the excess canvas to the back of the board and securing it with masking tape or by lacing the sides together (see page 125). Mount and frame the picture as required.

STITCH DETAILS

The roses in the lower left-hand corner of the picture are worked in three shades of pink and have bright yellow centers.

The garden path leads the eye to the back of the picture where there is a small garden bench worked in cream.

The supports of the arbor are worked in the charcoal yarn. They are covered in climbing roses on a background of blue and cream sky.

Viola picture

This design of a stylized viola is a miniature picture worked in simple cross-stitch on canvas.

Viola picture

YOU WILL NEED

- 4 × 4in 12-gauge single canvas
- Paternayan Persian yarn, one skein each of:

  Lilac 314   693 Bright green
  Dark green 691   727 Yellow
  Medium purple 302   300 Dark purple

- Tapestry needle

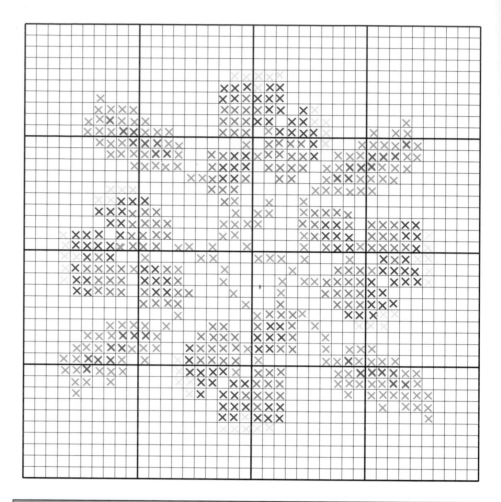

*T*his pretty design is quick to stitch and would make a thoughtful gift for someone who loves flowers and appreciates needlepoint.

The chart for the design is shown on the right. Each square represents one cross-stitch and shows which color to use. Fold the canvas lightly in half horizontally and vertically and mark the center lines. As the design is not symmetrical, mark the top of the canvas with a larger cross worked over two threads. This also helps you check that the "legs" of all the crosses are being worked in the same direction.

Using one strand of Paternayan Persian yarn in the needle throughout, begin stitching the green stems from the center outward. Then stitch the mauve and purple petals, tipping each one with yellow. Work a leaf in between each flower. Finally, fill in the background in pale mauve, working two stitches beyond each flower on the top, bottom, and right-hand edges and one stitch on the left-hand edge to make the design 36 stitches square.

HANGING THE PICTURE

When the viola picture is complete, you can mount and frame it (see page 125 for details on lacing the picture to a board). If you wish, you could make it into a large greeting card.

If you complete other floral pictures of the same size and mount them in identical frames, you could hang them on a satin or velvet ribbon to make an attractive set (see the box on the right for instructions).

bright idea

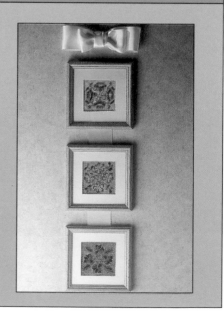

To hang a series of three pictures together you will need 1¾ yards of 2-inch wide satin ribbon, three D-rings and a curtain ring. First cut four lengths of ribbon, 26in, 16in, 10¼in and 4in long, respectively. Trim one end of the longer length into points – this is the piece of ribbon the pictures will hang on. For the bow, make two loops from the 16in long and 10¼in long pieces of ribbon and form them into a decorative bow. Wrap the 4in length around the center of the two loops and sew the bow to the top of the long length of ribbon. Attach the D-rings to the back of each picture and sew on to the ribbon. Sew the curtain ring to the back of the bow to hang the pictures.

Patio garden picture

*The vibrancy of bright summer flowers and shrubs is captured in
this pretty patio picture worked in half cross-stitch.*

Patio garden picture

YOU WILL NEED

- **12 × 14in 14-gauge single canvas**
- **Paternayan Persian yarn, one skein each of:**

Cream 261	444 Honey
Gray 202	771 Bright yellow
Pale olive 653	671 Lime green
Bright green 633	662 Pine green
Deep olive 651	664 Pale green
Sky blue 584	821 Red
Bright pink 961	301 Violet
Purple 331	321 Plum
Deep plum 320	460 Brown
	Rust 871

- **Two skeins of:**

  Beige gray 464
- **Tapestry needle**
- **7¼ × 9½in mounting board**

A sumptuous collection of garden flowers, combining tubs of geraniums, fuchsias, lilies, and lobelia with wall-climbing clematis and shrubs, brings the joy of high summer to this very pretty picture. A lavishly painted purple front door creates a focal point for the picture.

This patio scene is worked in bright outdoor colors and would complement a light, fresh interior – hung, for example, in a dining area or bedroom.

Embroidered in Paternayan Persian yarn on 14-gauge single canvas, the patio garden design is worked in half cross-stitch, using two strands of the yarn in the needle throughout. The finished picture measures 7¼ × 9½in. As the design is not too complicated and the areas of color are well-defined on the chart, this would be a very enjoyable project for a relative beginner to needlepoint.

BEFORE STITCHING

The design for the picture is given as a color chart on the opposite page. Each square on the chart represents one half cross-stitch. The key shows you which shade of Paternayan Persian yarn to use for each part of the picture.

To help you follow the chart, mark the vertical and horizontal center lines on the canvas with lines of basting stitches. Similarly, mark the corresponding center lines on the chart in pencil. These will give you useful reference points as you stitch, especially with an intricate design such as this, which uses a wide range of colors.

To help you find the colors as you need them, attach lengths of the yarn to a swatch card and mark each one with the skein color number. Swatch cards are available from craft stores or you can make your own by punching a row of holes along one side of a piece of cardboard.

Bind the raw edges of the canvas with masking tape to prevent the yarn from catching on them as you work, as this will cause the yarn to fray and become thin. Mount the prepared canvas in a scroll frame. This will

KEY

Paternayan Persian yarn, as used in the Patio garden picture:

	261 (A)		584 (K)
	444 (B)		821 (L)
	202 (C)		961 (M)
	771 (D)		301 (N)
	653 (E)		331 (O)
	671 (F)		321 (P)
	633 (G)		320 (Q)
	662 (H)		460 (R)
	651 (I)		871 (S)
	664 (J)		464 (T)

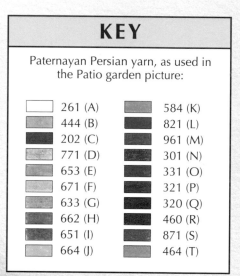

This swatch card shows the bright colors of Paternayan Persian yarn that are used to work the Patio garden picture. The key above right shows how they are used on the chart.

STITCH DETAILS

Interesting reflections of sky and clouds are worked behind the fanlight glazing bars. Embroider the clouds and sky first and then fill in the fanlight bars.

Potted plants are carefully placed to show the colored details. Notice how the shadows on the ground, stitched in horizontal lines, suggest the perspective of the path.

The flowers and leaves of the wall-climbing clematis are artistically grouped in a riot of color, setting off the deeper tone of the purple door behind them.

keep the canvas taut during stitching, which means that your stitches are all worked to the same tension, since using a frame allows you to work with both hands free so that you can stitch more quickly, with one hand on top and the other one below.

STITCHING THE DESIGN

Following the chart and color key given on the previous pages, work the patio garden design, starting in the middle of the canvas at your center point. For practical reasons, it is best to work darker colors first and lighter colors last – although you will find that yarn is more tolerant than floss, for example, in that it generally handles well and does not get dirty too quickly.

Where possible, it is best to start and finish one area of color before moving on to the next. To secure your yarn end when you begin, work the first few stitches over it; to finish off neatly, pass the needle through the last few stitches worked. Try to avoid carrying yarn across the back of your work as this causes unsightly lumps which can show on the right side, and the yarn may get caught up in the needle when you are working in another color.

As the picture builds up, you may find it helpful to have several needles threaded with the different colors in use. Those not actually being used can be pinned in the canvas margin. By completing small areas at a time,

and gradually building up the entire picture, you will find it less confusing than working colors at random. Take care, however, to keep the yarns not in use well away from your stitching area to avoid working over them.

FRAMING THE PICTURE

When the needlepoint is complete, remove the canvas from the frame and block it (see pages 103–4).

Mount the picture on a piece of firm mat board, folding the excess canvas to the wrong side of the board and securing it with masking tape. Alternatively, lace the canvas at the back of the mounting board (see page 125). Display it with or without a mat in the frame of your choice. Choose either a colored frame in a shade to match one of the yarn colors, or a simple wooden frame that complements the décor in your room.

Tubs of brightly colored geraniums and trailing lobelia are placed on the right-hand side of the garden path and draw your eye toward the center of the picture and the lavish purple of the front door.

Spring picture

*This view from a cottage window brings together all the vibrant colors
of spring painted in long stitch.*

Spring picture

YOU WILL NEED

- **12 × 14in 22-gauge single canvas**

- **Madeira 6-stranded floss, one skein each of:**

White	0103 Lemon
Yellow 0109	0106 Ocher
Pink 0503	0907 Sky blue
Pale blue 0908	1307 Bright green
Emerald 1213	1409 Yellow green
Olive green 1410	1209 Green-gray
Beige 2013	0101 Cream
Orange 0202	1911 Brown
Black	

- **Tapestry needle**

R olling green hills and sheep with their lambs give a peaceful rustic air to this springtime scene viewed through a country window. You can capture this piece of English countryside in fresh, crisp colors of 6-stranded Madeira embroidery floss on 22-count canvas, using one of the most versatile of needlepoint techniques – long stitch (see pages 115–6).

HOW TO BEGIN

The design for the spring picture is on the chart opposite and the trace pattern is on page 94. First, trace the pattern and then lay the canvas over the tracing. Transfer the design to the canvas using a pencil or a fabric marker pen. Then fold the canvas in half each way to find the center. Mount the canvas in a frame and you are ready to start. Work using six strands of floss unless specified.

Referring to the chart on the next page, start stitching the roof of the cottage at the center of the picture in vertical long stitch. Unless otherwise indicated on the color chart opposite, all the stitching is vertical.

BUILDING THE PICTURE

Work outward from the central point, stitching the hills in greens according to the chart. When you have completed this central pane of the window, stitch the frame around it, using horizontal stitching on the left and right sides, creating a chevron effect as you reach the points where the cross bars of the frame meet.

Continue working toward the edges, stitching the greenish-yellow bushes to the left of the cottage in sections as outlined to give a textured effect. It is this feature which makes long stitch so popular for pictures – because it is not an even-textured stitch like tent stitch or half cross-stitch, you can create shapes within an area of one color.

Where stitches would be too long if worked over the full extent of the color area, break them at a convenient point and stitch them in two moves (see pages 115–6). You will need to do this in the areas of the sky in the top left pane of the window , as shown in the detail, top right.

When you stitch the curtains, start at one end of a pleat at the curtain tie and work in

KEY

Madeira 6-stranded embroidery floss, as used in the Spring picture:

▦	White	▦	1410
▦	0101	▦	1213
▦	0103	▦	1409
▦	0109	▦	1307
▦	0106	▦	1209
▦	0202	▦	0907
▦	0503	▦	0908
▦	2013	╱	Straight stitch
▦	1911	⌐	Tiny straight st.
■	Black	●	French knot

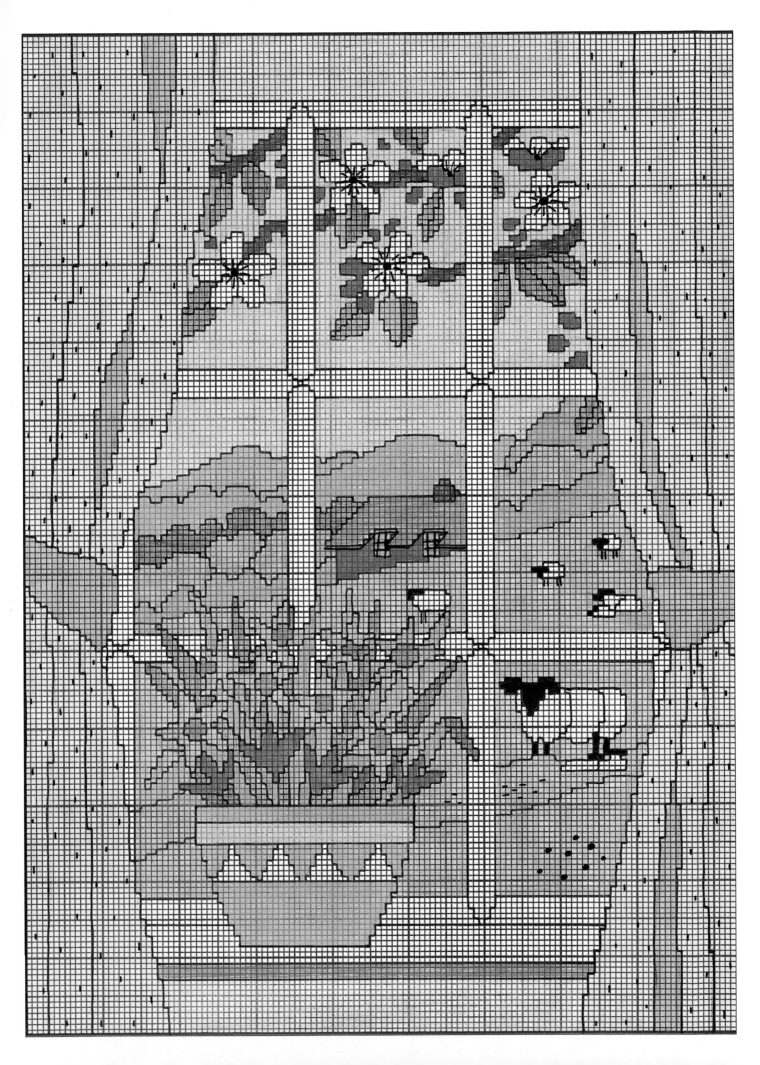

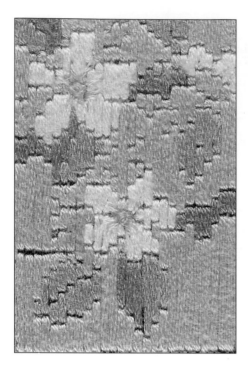

horizontal stitches right up that strip until you reach the top of the design. Repeat this with the rest of the pleats, working up or down from the curtain ties. Make sure, when abutting horizontal stitches to vertical ones, that you cover the canvas completely (see pages 115–6), working into the hole directly beneath the stitch at right angles.

FINISHING TOUCHES

When you have stitched the whole design, you can add some details – these are shown only in black on the stitching chart, but appear on the framed picture. Use two strands of medium yellow to add the stamen in the centers of the apple blossom flowers, then work a French knot in the center of each in three strands of deep yellow as in the detail above. To complete the design, add a dot pattern on the curtains in cream (as in the detail, center right) and work French knots in ocher below the sheep in the lower right-hand corner of the window (detail, bottom left) and latticework on the cottage windows in black, as shown in the detail, bottom right.

When the picture is complete, remove it from the frame. Long stitch does not tend to distort, but you may find that your picture needs pulling into shape before your frame it. If this is the case, follow the steps on page 103–4 for blocking and stretching, or take it to a specialist to get it blocked and mounted.

STITCH DETAILS

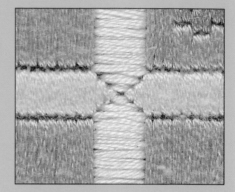

Break up stitches which would otherwise be too long by interlocking stitches in a common hole. This is necessary where the blue of the sky is unbroken along the sides of the top left-hand window pane.

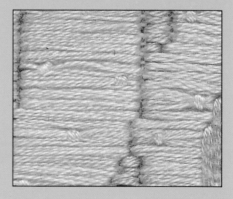

When you abut horizontal and vertical stitches, as where the curtains and the landscape meet, make sure that the horizontal stitches cover the vertical threads of canvas under the vertical stitches.

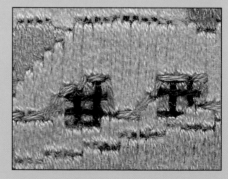

Use three strands of ocher floss to work a scattering of French knots in the grass just below the sheep in the foreground. Just above this, to the left, add a few random seed stitches to represent small flowers.

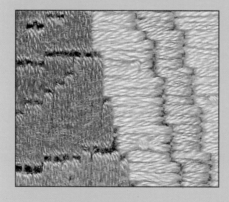

Where the vertical and horizontal stitches on the window frame meet, work them so they meet in neat, diagonal lines, giving a mitered effect at the intersection of the pieces of the frame.

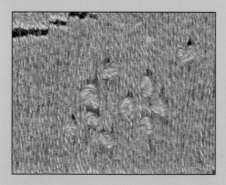

Still using all six strands of cream floss, add a random dot pattern on the curtains, working small vertical stitches over just one thread of canvas. Be careful not to pull the stitches too tightly.

Using three strands of black floss, add the lattice detail to the windows of the cottage. This detailing completes the picture, which is now ready to stretch and frame as you wish.

Geometric mirror case

This stylish needlepoint mirror case has a very smart design and will protect
a small rectangular mirror inside your purse.

Geometric mirror case

YOU WILL NEED

- 3½ × 4½in 16-gauge single canvas
- Paternayan Persian yarn, one skein each of:

  Pale blue 503   501 Blue

  Lilac 322   840 Red

  Gold 701   D500 Green

  Purple 320

- Tapestry needle
- 3½ × 4½in pale blue cotton-blend fabric
- Pale blue sewing thread
- Sewing needle

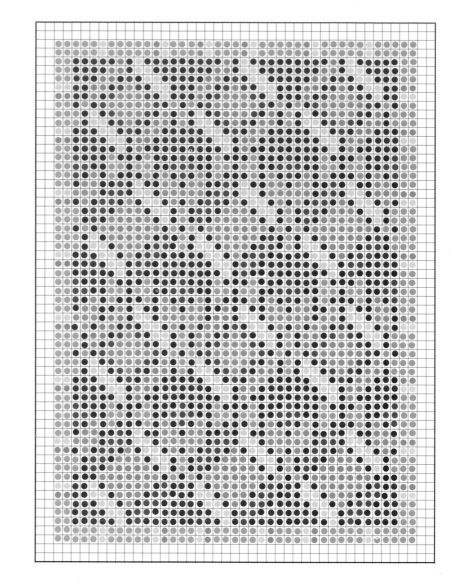

The bright colors of this mirror case are reminiscent of the traditional diamond-patterned clothes of a harlequin, with the checks and diagonal stripes stitched in contrasting red, yellow, green, lilac, and blue.

The wool yarn used for the design is strong and yet soft, making it both hardwearing and also very suitable for protecting a mirror. It measures 2¾ x 3½ inches so will fit an average-sized mirror.

BEGIN STITCHING

Fold the canvas in half each way and mark the center with lines of basting. Mark the center of the chart in pencil. Follow the chart on the right to stitch the geometric design. Make sure that you have enough canvas around each edge to turn under when finishing the mirror case.

Begin by working the blue and yellow border, creating a frame within which to work and allowing you to position the design centrally on your canvas.

The design is worked in tent stitch, which gives a firm finish. Stitch the design in blocks of color, but do not stretch long strands of yarn across the back of the canvas.

FINISHING

Once the stitching is finished, stretch your canvas back into a perfect rectangle (see pages 103–4). Finish any loose ends on the back of your work by darning them under a few stitches.

Trim excess canvas away from the corners, making sure not to clip too close to the stitching. Fold the spare canvas under on each side of the rectangle and press firmly. Secure one short end of the canvas down on the wrong side using tiny oversewing stitches.

Press under the raw edges around the two long sides and one short end of the cotton-blend backing fabric and slip stitch it neatly to the needlepoint. Make a double hem at the top of the cotton-blend fabric to finish the mirror case.

finishing touches

Make a lining by cutting a piece of fabric the same width as the mirror case but twice as long, plus allowances. Stitch three sides to make a pocket and turn a hem at the top. Slide the lining into the mirror case and attach it to the design by slipstitching the top edges together.

Tissue box cover

This needlepoint cover for a tissue box is a useful and decorative accessory for a bedroom or bathroom.

Tissue box cover

Show off your needlepoint skills with this tissue box cover in two shades of turquoise. Long stitch is used to create a basketweave effect in the center of each side and this is surrounded with borders of half cross-stitch, Smyrna stitch, and long stitch. The top of the box has the same border pattern, but the center is cut out to match the hole in the tissue box. All four sides and the top are worked on one piece of canvas, and the panels are then folded and stitched into the box shape. As worked canvas forms a firm fabric, the box will hold its shape well. The cover fits an average cube-shaped tissue box – about 4¾in along on each side. However, it can be adapted to accommodate larger boxes by elongating the rows of stitching in the borders and extending the basketweave pattern.

CHARTS FOR THE BOX SHAPE

Chart 1 opposite shows the stitch pattern for the side panels and Chart 2 shows the stitch pattern and the central cut-out for the top of the box. The lines of the grid represent the canvas threads. The diagram of how the panels are pieced together is shown on page 95. The number of stitches along each side of the panels and top is indicated where relevant. To help you with positioning the panels correctly, count the canvas threads and mark the outline of the box on the canvas with lines of basting thread.

STITCHING THE TISSUE BOX COVER

Mount the canvas in a scroll frame before you begin stitching to prevent it from distorting. Using two strands of Persian yarn in the needle, begin by stitching panel A as shown in the diagram on page 95. Secure your yarn at the back by working the first few stitches over it, and finish off by running the needle under the last few stitches. Using Chart 1, find the center point of the panel and start stitching

YOU WILL NEED

- **15 × 24in 12-gauge single canvas**
- **Paternayan Persian yarn, four skeins of:**
  Medium turquoise 593
- **Five skeins of:**
  Pale turquoise 594
- **Tapestry needle**
- **Sewing thread**

the central square in half cross-stitch (page 125) in medium turquoise (593).

Complete all the other squares of half cross-stitch, counting the canvas threads carefully as you move from one to the other. Then work the basketweave pattern in horizontal and vertical long stitch (pages 115–6) in pale turquoise (594). Next work the long stitch border around the basketweave pattern in pale turquoise, mitering the stitching at the corners. Hide any canvas threads which show where the two patterns meet with a line of backstitch in medium turquoise. Work a narrow border of half cross-stitch in medium turquoise, a wide border of long stitch in pale turquoise, and a border of Smyrna stitch (see pages 123–4) in medium turquoise. Note how the center of each row of Smyrna stitch is worked in half cross-stitch. Finish with a row of half cross-stitch in pale turquoise at top and bottom. Just for panel A, omit the row of half cross-stitch on the left-hand side, as indicated on Chart 1. The row of half cross-stitch shown on the right-hand side of the chart in green indicates where the pattern begins to repeat at the vertical edge.

Now work panel B next to panel A. You might prefer to work the borders from the outside toward the center to avoid having to count out too many threads. When you reach the basketweave pattern, stitch the small half cross-stitch squares and then the basketweave in long stitch. At the top edge of panel B, work

This side of the box shows how two harmonizing colors have been used to create a shadow on the basketweave pattern.

CHART 1 – PANELS A, B, C AND D

OMIT THIS ROW ON PANEL A

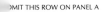

CENTER

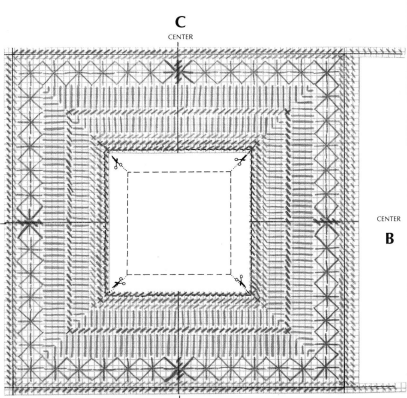

CENTER — CENTER

CENTER

56 STITCHES

CHART 2 – TOP E

C

CENTER

CENTER — CENTER

D   **B**

CENTER

A

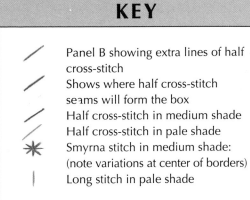

	KEY
/	Panel B showing extra lines of half cross-stitch
/	Shows where half cross-stitch seams will form the box
/	Half cross-stitch in medium shade
/	Half cross-stitch in pale shade
✳	Smyrna stitch in medium shade: (note variations at center of borders)
|	Long stitch in pale shade

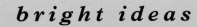

bright ideas

Why not make this tissue box cover to match your bedroom or bathroom? We have used two turquoise shades of Paternayan Persian yarn – 593 for the medium shade and 594 for the pale one – but you could use any colors. Remember to keep them quite close in shade to achieve the right effect.

The two mauves shown here would be perfect for a cool color scheme. The Paternayan Persian yarn used is 543 for the medium shade and 546 for the pale shade.

Pink is always popular for a feminine look. Here we have used 911 for the medium shade and 914 for the pale shade.

Use two shades of yellow for a bright summery look. The medium shade shown is 912 and the pale shade is 913.

63

HOW TO FINISH THE TISSUE BOX COVER

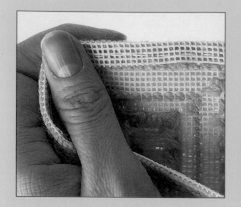

1 *Turn up a hem of about five canvas threads all around the bottom edge of the box shape and secure with small, neat running stitches in strong sewing thread.*

2 *Join the upright seam using a vertical row of half cross-stitches, making sure that all the holes align – marking the holes at regular intervals will give reference points.*

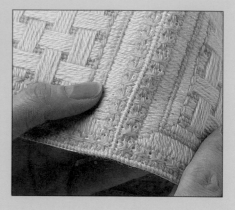

3 *When the upright seam has been stitched, it should provide an exact match for the fold lines that have been worked on the other three sides.*

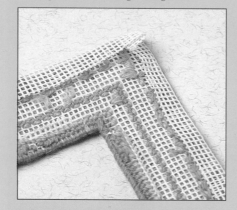

4 *Turn up a hem of about five canvas threads all around the three free sides of the box top. Fold under excess fabric at the corners and baste in position.*

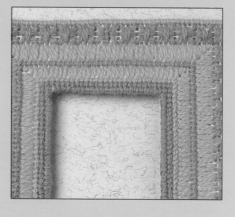

5 *The allowances along the top edge should run exactly parallel with the stitched edge. If this edge is not straight, some of the canvas may show through when the seam is joined.*

6 *To complete the box, use half cross-stitch to join the sides of the box top to the top edges of each side. When stitching, make sure that the holes align.*

an extra row of half cross-stitch as this is where the top panel E is connected. Work panels C and D as for panel B, but omit the second row of half cross-stitch at the top edge.

Now work the box top E, following Chart 2. Work the borders from the outside in. Note the lines of half cross-stitch in the center of the Smyrna stitch rows, as for the side panels. Before you stitch the inner three rows of half cross-stitch, cut out the central area of canvas for the hole as shown, leaving turnings of three canvas threads and snipping diagonally into the corners. You may find it helps to prevent the edges from fraying if you put masking tape over the corners to be clipped and then cut through the tape. Remove the tape just

before you need to stitch the corners. Turn this unworked canvas under and work the inner three rows of half cross-stitch through both layers to give a neat finished edge.

FINISHING THE COVER

When all the panels are complete, take the needlepoint off the frame and block it if necessary (see pages 103–4). Cut out around the box shape, leaving seam allowances of five canvas threads as shown on page 95.

Turn a small hem under at the bottom of the box, securing it in position with small running stitches, using strong cotton thread. Press the seam allowances with an iron if necessary. Then fold along the lines indicated

on page 95, pressing with your fingers to form a firm edge along each line of half cross-stitch. Also fold along the extra line of half cross-stitch at the top edge of panel B.

The steps above show how to finish the box. Start to assemble the box by joining the upright seam in the box sides with half cross-stitch (this row replaces the row skipped when originally stitching panel A). Fold under the seam allowances on the side panels and on the top; then using two strands of pale turquoise, join the panels to the top with half cross-stitch. Make sure the holes are all in line so each stitch can be worked through both pieces of canvas and the edges will be equal. Place the cover over the tissue box.

Cat door-stop

*Irresistible to all cat-lovers, this winsome tabby, stitched in needlepoint,
will look decorative while holding your door open for you.*

Cat door-stop

Needlepoint is used here in an unusual and original way to make a decorative door-stop in the shape of a cat. Made as a three-dimensional figure, it is so realistic that you might mistake it for the real thing! The fur is worked in tent stitch in shades of gray and fawn, and its whiskers are added later in fine split stitch. To complete the effect, it has soulful blue eyes and a delicate pink nose. The pink bow around the cat's neck is trimmed with a brass bell on a real ribbon.

So that the door-stop is heavy, it is filled with a cotton bag containing a piece of brick and some sand, although you could use any heavy weight. The design is worked in tent stitch and stands 13¼ inches tall.

STITCHING THE DESIGN

Bind the raw edges of the canvas with masking tape before you begin stitching. As tent stitch tends to distort the canvas, mount it on a scroll frame to keep it in shape (see page 125). Mark the horizontal and vertical center lines of the canvas with lines of basting and mark the center of the chart in pencil to help you to position the cat centrally.

The color chart for the cat is shown on the opposite page. Each square on the chart represents one tent stitch. Follow the key for the colors. Using two strands of yarn in the needle, begin stitching centrally, finishing off one area of color before starting the next.

Work the cream and fawn areas of the cat's "bib" first, adding a few patches of pale gray. Then stitch the ribbon and bow in the two darker shades of pink. Work up from here to the head, on which the colors graduate from cream and fawn to patches of dark, medium and pale gray. The eyes are stitched in turquoise yarn with black outlines, and the nose and ear centers are worked in pale pink.

Now work the top part of the body to the left of the "bib" in three shades of gray, introducing fawn and cream into the lower part of the body where the legs and tail are stitched.

When you have finished the tent stitch, add the whiskers in split stitch (see page 125) in cream, using one strand of Persian yarn. These extend outward and down from the

nose area and upward at the ears. When the stitching is complete, remove from the frame and, if necessary, block your canvas (see page 103–4).

FINISHING THE CAT

Trim the canvas from around the cat to within ½ inch of the stitched area. Cut a piece of velvet to the same shape, with the pile running downward. Pin the two pieces together with right sides facing. Machine stitch or backstitch around the outline, close to the worked edge. Turn the cat right side out, pushing out the ears and curves with a blunt point. Trace the base pattern on page 96 and use it to cut out one base from the velvet. With right sides facing, stitch it to the lower edge of the cat with a ½-inch seam. Trim and clip the curves.

To make the weighted bag, cut two rectangles 6 x 8¼ inches from heavy cotton fabric. Also cut a base using the trace pattern. Make the weighted bag following the instructions overleaf. Stuff the head and neck of the cat with batting. Insert the weighted bag and fill the rest of the cat with batting. Close the opening at the base. Loop the ribbon through the bell and sew onto the cat's stitched bow.

YOU WILL NEED

- **16 × 20in 14-gauge interlock canvas**

- **Paternayan Persian yarn (no. of skeins in brackets):**

  (1) Turquoise 584   961 Bright pink *(1)*
  (1) Medium pink 963   935 Pale pink *(1)*
  (1) Black   202 Pale gray *(2)*
  (2) Cream 261   405 Fawn *(3)*
  (3) Med. gray D346   210 Dark gray *(6)*

- **Tapestry needle**

- **⅜yd of 36in-wide gray velvet**

- **12 × 12in heavy cotton fabric**

- **Small brass bell (optional)**

- **Scrap of narrow pink ribbon (optional)**

- **Synthetic batting and sand**

- **Large weight or small brick**

KEY

Paternayan Persian yarn as used in the Cat door-stop:

- Turquoise (584)
- Pale pink (935)
- Bright pink (961)
- Med. pink (963)
- Black
- Med. gray (D346)
- Pale gray (202)
- Fawn (405)
- Cream (261)
- Dark gray (210)

HOW TO MAKE THE WEIGHTED BAG

 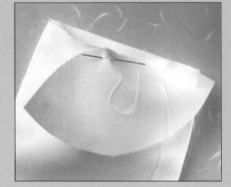 

1 Cut out two rectangles and a base from heavy cotton fabric. You will also need a small brick and some fine, light-colored sand for the weight. Sandbox sand is ideal as it is clean and soft.

2 Using small, tight stitches to prevent the sand from leaking out, machine-stitch or backstitch the sides and the top of the bag together. Attach one side of the base with a small, firm backstitch.

3 Place a small amount of sand in the bottom of the bag and then add the small brick. Fill in around the brick with the sand until the bag is firm and heavy. Slipstitch the open side tightly.

bright idea

KEY

Paternayan Persian yarn as used in the Cat door-stop:

- For turquoise (584) use teal blue (522)
- For pale pink (935) use flesh pink (492)
- For bright pink (961) use dark green (501)
- For mid pink (963) use mid green (503)
- For mid gray (D346) use ginger (722)
- For pale gray (202) use pale orange (805)
- For fawn (405) use cinnamon (D423)
- For cream (261) use cream (263)
- For dark gray (210) use dark ginger (880)
- For black use black

Make this smiling cat in shades of ginger to be a furry companion to the tabby by changing the colors as shown on the chart. The key shows you which yarns to substitute for the original ones. Replace the colors in the same way throughout, following the main chart.

Hall bench cushion

*Bargello embroidery in a variety of diamond shapes is used
to great effect on this rectangular seat cover.*

Hall bench cushion

YOU WILL NEED

- **30 × 32in 12-gauge single canvas**
- **Paternayan Persian yarn (no. of skeins in brackets):**

  (*1*) Brown 440   863 Pale rust (*2*)
  (*2*) Medium rust 862   442 Ocher (*2*)
  (*5*) Pale blue 515   732 Gold (*5*)
  (*6*) Dark rust 860   734 Pale gold (*6*)
  (*7*) Dark blue 510   513 Medium blue (*7*)
  (*10*) Dark green 520

- **Tapestry needle**
- **15 × 26in backing fabric**
- **13½ × 24in piece of 2in-deep foam for filling**
- **2¼yd gold twisted satin cord**
- **Sewing needle and thread**

Bold shades of gold, orange, blue, and green form diamonds within diamonds on this stunning cushion, which is worked in bargello embroidery (see also pages 17–20). Gusset strips worked in a different pattern are set into the sides to form a box shape that is ideal to cover a hall seat or bench.

The finished design measures 13½ × 24 inches and the sides are 2 inches deep. The rich colors would look perfect with wood and will suit most room settings.

BEFORE YOU START

Cut a piece of canvas measuring 17½ × 30in for the top of the cushion – the remaining piece will be for the side panels. Bind the edges of both pieces of canvas with masking tape or bias binding, making sure that the raw edges are well covered. Fold the canvas in half each way and mark the horizontal and vertical centers with lines of basting. Mount the canvas in a scroll frame to keep the stitches taut while you work. This will ensure that the design has a neat, professional-looking finish.

STITCHING THE TOP PANEL

The top of the cushion is worked in a large diamond pattern, which is formed by first working an overall grid using the dark green yarn (520). Start in the center of the marked canvas, following the chart on the right and using the key on the right and the swatch card on the left to keep track of the colors. Work outward until the grid measures 17½ × 24 inches, ending with either a full or half diamond at the edges. Use three strands of the yarn in the needle.

When the dark green grid has been worked to the required size, fill in the gold, blue, and orange patterns within each large diamond. The majority of these stitches are worked over

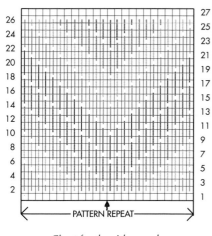

Chart for the side panels

KEY

Paternayan Persian yarn, as used
in the Hall bench cushion:

—————	Dark rust – 860 (A)
—————	Medium rust – 862 (B)
—————	Pale rust – 863 (C)
—————	Ochre – 442 (D)
—————	Dark green – 520 (E)
—————	Pale gold – 734 (F)
—————	Gold – 732 (G)
—————	Brown – 440 (H)
—————	Dark blue – 510 (I)
—————	Medium blue – 513 (J)
—————	Pale blue – 515 (K)

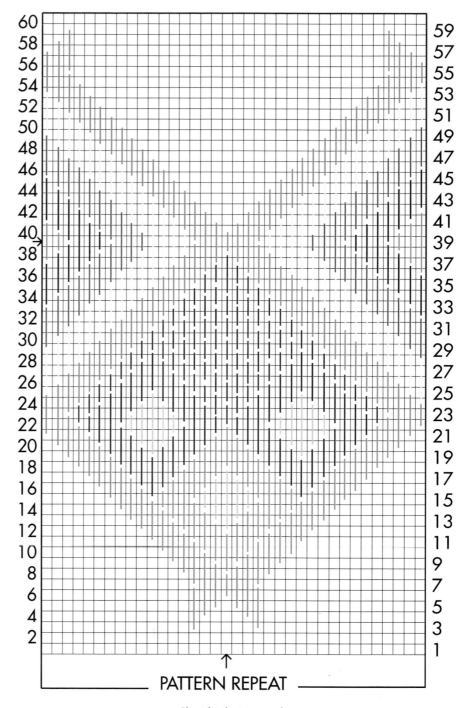

Chart for the top panel

four canvas threads, with smaller stitches used
to fill in the gaps. Take care when you are
working that all the stitches are made to the
correct length as shown on the charts and that
they share common holes in the canvas. In
this way the canvas will be properly covered
and no gaps will appear.

WORKING THE SIDE PANELS

Use two strands of the yarn in the needle for
the side panels. Starting with the longer side
pieces, follow the small chart above to work
two strips, each 2 x 24 inches. Begin in the
center of the strips and work out to the sides
so the pattern will balance at the side seam
edges. Make sure when you are working these
pieces that you leave at least 1⅛ inches
between each one for seam allowances.

For the end pieces, follow the same chart
and work two strips, each 2 x 13½ inches.
You may need to work slightly more or fewer
stitches so that the pattern matches at the

corners, giving the impression of one long
continuous strip.

FINISHING THE CUSHION

Press the five pieces very carefully from the
wrong side over a lightly padded surface. This
will prevent the stitches from becoming flat-
tened. Trim the excess canvas from around
the pieces to leave a ½-inch seam allowance.

With right sides facing, backstitch or
machine stitch the top edges of the side pieces

to the outer edges of the top panel. Slipstitch
the corners to create a box shape, leaving the
left back corner open. With right sides facing,
stitch the backing fabric to the lower edges of
the side pieces, but leave one short end open.
Clip across the corners to remove excess
canvas. Turn right side out. Insert the piece of
foam through the open end and slipstitch to
close. Slipstitch the cord around the top edge
of the cushion, inserting the ends into the left
back corner to hide them.

ALTERNATIVE COLORS

The two sets of twisted skeins on this page show the way in which the colors used to work this design can be changed to match your décor. When you wish to alter the colors of a design an any way, it is important that the balance between them is maintained. For example, in this design, you will need one very dark color to work the diamond grid and then another ten colors that can be split into one group of four and two groups of three. Within these groups, the colors should be different shades of one color, with enough definition between them so that the overall effect will not be lost.

If you can, try out your chosen colors on a spare piece of canvas first to check that you have the right balance between them. If this is not feasible, use a piece of graph paper and colored pencils or pens that match your yarn colors as well as possible, and draw the design. This will give a rough indication of the final effect and may be enough to show you if one or more colors are not working correctly.

It is possible to create a more delicate effect with this pattern simply by changing the gauge of the canvas and the number of strands of yarn used. For example, use two strands on 14-gauge canvas or even one strand on 18-gauge canvas to reduce the scale of the design quite considerably.

PINK AND PURPLE COMBINATION

This variation uses very soft heathery colors to give a Scottish feel to the design. It would look perfect with dark wood furniture in a traditional room setting.

For this color combination, use the very dark plum (320) to replace the dark green used for the original. The remaining colors then split up into three groups. Replace the shades of gold in the original design with the four shades of pink (903, 905, 914, and 326) using the darkest shade in the center of the diamond. For the three blues, use the plum shades (321, 322, and 324). Finally, replace the three shades of rust with the three lavender colors (D147, D127, and D117). Avoid placing the darkest color in each group next to the very dark plum of the grid, as the colors are similar.

GREEN AND BLUE COMBINATION

This variation uses very cool shades that would look perfect in a more modern setting, perhaps with simple pine furniture.

First, use the very dark blue (500) to replace the dark green grid on the original design. For the four colors originally used to work the gold diamonds, use the four shades of green (D556, D546, 522, and D516). Make sure that the darkest shade is worked in the center of the diamond so that it does not clash with the very dark blue of the grid. The three shades of blue (502, 503, and 505) can be used in place of the three shades of rust in the original design. Finally use the three grays (210, 211, and 213) to replace the three blue colors.

KEY

Paternayan Persian yarn, as used in the pink and purple combination:

- **A** Very pale lavender (D147)
- **B** Pale plum (324)
- **C** Dark lavender (D117)
- **D** Dark plum (321)
- **E** Very dark plum (320)
- **F** Medium lavender (D127)
- **G** Medium plum (322)
- **H** Bright pink (903)
- **I** Medium pink (905)
- **J** Pale pink (914)
- **K** Very pale pink (326)

KEY

Paternayan Persian yarn, as used in the green and blue combination:

- **A** Very pale gray (213)
- **B** Pale sea green (D556)
- **C** Medium sea green (D546)
- **D** Medium leaf green (522)
- **E** Dark sea green (D516)
- **F** Very dark blue (500)
- **G** Dark gray (210)
- **H** Medium gray (211)
- **I** Dark blue (502)
- **J** Medium blue (503)
- **K** Pale blue (505)

Floral rug

A host of summer flowers on a trellis background fill
the center of this needlepoint cross-stitch rug.

Floral rug

YOU WILL NEED

- **30 × 44in 7-gauge rug canvas**

- **Paternayan Persian yarn (number of skeins required given in brackets) in the following colors:**

(*1*) Bright yellow 772	544 Sky blue (*2*)
(*2*) Mauve blue 342	554 Pale blue (*3*)
(*3*) Strawberry 952	715 Pale yellow (*4*)
(*4*) Dusty pink 911	906 Sugar pink (*8*)
(*8*) Forest green 602	694 Pale green (*8*)
(*10*) Cream 263	612 Bright green (*10*)
(*10*) Rose pink 904	513 Gray blue (*11*)
(*15*) Pale pink 964	511 Dk gray blue (*62*)

- **Tapestry needle**

- **30 × 44in burlap for backing**

- **Slate frame (optional)**

Create a family heirloom with this pretty rug decorated with a profusion of summer flowers. A trellis pattern in two shades of gray-blue fills the background. The rug is easy to work in cross-stitch on a large-gauge canvas and would be perfect for use as a bedside or hearthside rug.

KEY

Paternayan Persian yarn, as used in the Floral rug:

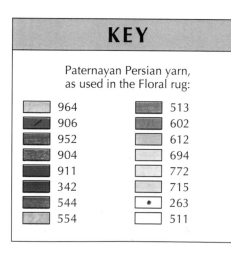

964	513
906	602
952	612
904	694
911	772
342	715
544	263
554	511

The chart for this design has been split into two, to allow it to be shown as large as possible. No overlap has been allowed between the pieces, and the chart should be followed as usual.

A wide variety of colors has been used to create a very realistic effect when working the flowers, but if you wish, the background color could be changed to match your décor. Try to avoid very pale colors, though, as they may detract from the pink roses and will not be as practical as a darker one.

BEFORE YOU START

Bind the edges of the canvas with either bias binding or masking tape, making sure that they are well covered. Fold the canvas in half and then in half again and mark the center with horizontal and vertical lines of basting. Use sewing thread, which can be worked over and then removed when the design is complete. Mark the corresponding center of the chart on the previous pages with a pencil.

Mount the canvas in a scroll frame. This will help keep your stitching neat and even, and you will find it much easier to work a canvas of this size if it is stretched in a frame as it will allow you to concentrate on specific areas of the design.

STITCHING THE DESIGN

The rug is worked in cross-stitch, using three strands of yarn in the needle throughout. Start stitching at the center points of the chart and the canvas. To start an area of color, leave a short end on the wrong side that can be worked over by

bright idea

If you wish to give your completed rug a more professional finish, you could fringe the short ends. This could be worked in any of the yarn colors, but will look best in the dark gray-blue used for the background. You will also need a latch tool as used for hooked rugs or a large crochet hook, with which to pull the yarn through the holes in the canvas. You will need to buy four extra skeins of yarn. Cut the yarn into lengths of about 15in. Fold into two and then hook through alternate holes along the edges of the canvas.

the first few stitches. Finish off neatly by passing the needle back through a few stitches on the back of the work.

Work the central spray first, then fill in the lines of the trellis pattern in gray blue (513). The background should be worked last in dark gray blue (511). When all the cross-stitching is complete, check that you have not missed any stitches, as these will be very difficult to add

once the rug has been completed. Finish any loose ends on the back of the canvas that may prevent the rug from lying flat when it is complete.

FINISHING THE RUG

Remove the canvas from the frame and block it if necessary (see pages 103–4). Cut the burlap backing so that it is just 2¼ inches bigger each way than the finished needlepoint. Turn 1⅛ inches under along each edge and press firmly in position. Turn the excess canvas around the design to the wrong side and catch down. Slipstitch the backing fabric in place around the edges.

KEY

Paternayan Persian yarn, as used in the Floral rug:

Ⓐ 964	Ⓔ 911	Ⓘ 513	Ⓜ 772
Ⓑ 906	Ⓕ 342	Ⓙ 602	Ⓝ 715
Ⓒ 952	Ⓖ 544	Ⓚ 612	Ⓞ 263
Ⓓ 904	Ⓗ 554	Ⓛ 694	Ⓟ 511

Ⓐ Ⓑ Ⓒ Ⓓ Ⓔ Ⓕ Ⓖ Ⓗ Ⓘ Ⓙ Ⓚ Ⓛ Ⓜ Ⓝ Ⓞ Ⓟ

Shelduck pillow

Make this appealing needlepoint duck into a shaped pillow,
and he will always get a second glance.·

Shelduck pillow

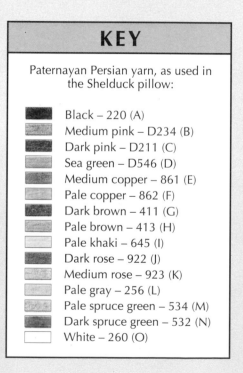

This delightful character is a shelduck, a species which inhabits the sand dunes and tidal mud-flats of European coastal areas. He has handsome plumage with a white body and muted green head and wing markings. A band of copper enlivens his chest coloring, and his beak, legs, and webbed feet are a beautiful soft pink. His beady black eyes have a white highlight to give them a realistic sparkle. The shelduck is shown set against the water plants of his accustomed habitat and would make an unusual and witty addition to a collection of pillows in a child's room.

The shelduck pillow is worked entirely in tent stitch, which gives it a strong finish and a firm texture. It measures 10 inches high by 10 inches wide.

BEFORE YOU BEGIN

The chart for the shelduck design is shown on the opposite page. Each colored square equals one tent stitch, and the colors of yarn to use are given in the key and on the swatch card below.

Bind the raw edges of the canvas with masking tape to prevent the yarn from snagging on them and wearing thin. If this happens, it is irritating, and thin yarn may not cover the canvas.

To help you when you are following the chart, it is a good idea to mark the center of both the chart and the canvas. Fold the canvas lightly in half each way and mark the center with lines of basting. These can be worked over and removed, if necessary, when the design is finished. Mark the center lines on the chart in pencil to correspond.

As tent stitch is a strongly diagonal stitch, it tends to pull the canvas out of shape as you are stitching. To prevent this from happening, stretch the canvas in a scroll frame to keep it taut as you are stitching (see page 125). This will give a smoother, more professional-looking finish, and will also speed up your stitching, as you can work with one hand held above and one below the canvas, passing the needle through from one side to the other with a stabbing motion. It is important to keep the outline of a shaped pillow from being distorted, as you may find it more difficult to restore it to its correct shape than a square or rectangular pillow.

STITCHING THE SHELDUCK

The pillow is stitched using two strands of yarn in the needle throughout. As some of the shades of green, copper, and pink are quite close, you may find it helpful to organize your skeins of yarn onto swatch cards, which you can purchase from craft stores or even make

YOU WILL NEED

- **14 × 14in 12-gauge single canvas**
- **Paternayan Persian yarn, one skein each of:**

Pale brown 413	411 Dark brown
Black 220	532 Dark spruce
Pale spruce 534	256 Pale gray
Dark rose 922	923 Medium rose
Pale copper 862	861 Medium copper
Medium pink D234	D211 Dark pink
Sea green D546	

- **Two skeins of:**
  White 260
- **Three skeins of:**
  Pale khaki 645
- **Tapestry needle**
- **14 × 14in backing fabric**
- **Synthetic toy stuffing**

KEY

Paternayan Persian yarn, as used in the Shelduck pillow:

- Black – 220 (A)
- Medium pink – D234 (B)
- Dark pink – D211 (C)
- Sea green – D546 (D)
- Medium copper – 861 (E)
- Pale copper – 862 (F)
- Dark brown – 411 (G)
- Pale brown – 413 (H)
- Pale khaki – 645 (I)
- Dark rose – 922 (J)
- Medium rose – 923 (K)
- Pale gray – 256 (L)
- Pale spruce green – 534 (M)
- Dark spruce green – 532 (N)
- White – 260 (O)

Use the chart above and the key and swatch card on the page opposite to work the Shelduck pillow. Each colored square represents one tent stitch using two strands of yarn.

yourself from strips of cardboard. Punch holes along the edges of the cardboard and loop the yarn through them. Mark the name and number beside each one and it will be easier to find each color as you need it.

Following the chart carefully, begin stitching the duck centrally. To secure your yarn at the beginning, leave a short length at the back of the canvas and work the first few stitches over it. To finish off, pass the needle under the last few stitches worked at the back and cut the end off short. Start by stitching the duck's chest in white (260) with pale gray (256) and pale khaki (645) feather markings. Work in blocks of color, finishing one shade before starting the next, and remember not to take long strands across the back from one part of the design to another.

Continue the duck's body by working the bright band across the chest in two shades of copper with pale brown (413) at the edges. Pale brown also outlines the lower part of the body. Now stitch the mottled plumage of the wing in four different colors – dark spruce green (532), pale spruce green (534), dark brown (411), and black (220). Add another copper-colored marking just below the wing. The head is worked in two shades of spruce green with eyes in black and white. The distinctive beak is dark pink (D211) and medium pink (D234) with black shading and white highlights.

When the duck's body is complete, fill in his legs in dark rose (922) and medium rose (923) with dark brown shading. The plants are in dark spruce green and sea green (D546). Finally, work the background in pale khaki.

FINISHING THE PILLOW

Remove the needlepoint from the frame. If it needs to be restored to shape, block it as described pages 103–4. Trim excess canvas around the duck shape to ½ inch all around. Cut a piece of backing fabric to match.

With right sides facing, pin the backing fabric to the needlepoint. Sew together with backstitch, leaving the lower edge open. Work close to the edge of the needlepoint so that no canvas threads will show when the pillow is turned right side out. Notch the seams to reduce bulk so that they will lie flat.

Turn right side out, pushing out the head with a large crochet hook or blunt implement. Fill with stuffing, pushing it well up into the head. Turn in the raw edges along the lower edge and slipstitch to close.

STITCH DETAILS

The duck's head is worked in harmonizing shades of spruce green and the beak in soft shades of pink. His chest is worked in white with pale khaki and pale gray details.

The mottled plumage on the duck's back is suggested by clever shaping worked in an attractive combination of spruce greens with black and dark brown.

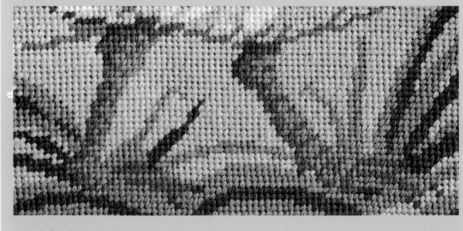

Stitch the shelduck's legs and webbed feet in two shades of rose with dark brown claws and shading. The reeds are in spruce and sea green, and the background is pale khaki.

Noah's Ark picture

Brighten up a child's bedroom with this jolly picture
of Noah and some of the animals in his Ark.

Noah's Ark picture

Any child would love this colorful needlepoint picture to hang up in his or her bedroom. It depicts Noah standing proudly on his Ark with some of the animals he has rescued from the flood. A rainbow above the Ark signifies the end of the rain, and the dove of peace carrying its olive branch flutters in from the right-hand corner.

As the needlepoint is worked in half cross-stitch throughout, this is not a difficult project for even a beginner to try. Bright shades of Paternayan Persian yarn have been used to make a bold design, and some of these have been blended to create subtle mixed colors.

For maximum impact, set the picture into a primary-colored frame with a plain white mat. The finished size of the needlepoint is 12 inches high by 12½ inches wide.

BEFORE YOU BEGIN

The chart for the Noah's Ark design is shown on the opposite page. Each colored square equals one half cross-stitch, and the colors of yarn to use are given in the key opposite and the swatch card below left. Bind the raw edges of the canvas with masking tape to prevent the yarn from snagging on them and wearing thin. If this happens, the yarn may not cover the canvas properly.

To help you when you are following the chart, mark the center of both the chart and the canvas. Fold the canvas lightly in half each way and mark the center with lines of basting, which, if necessary, can be worked over and removed when you have finished the needlepoint. Mark the center lines on the chart in pencil to correspond.

It would be wise to stretch the canvas in a scroll frame to keep it taut as you are stitching (see page 125). This will give a smoother, more professional-looking finish, and will also help you to speed up your stitching, as you can work with one hand held above and one below the canvas, passing the needle through from·one side to the other with a stabbing motion.

STITCHING THE PICTURE

The picture is stitched entirely in half cross-stitch, using two strands of yarn in the needle. You will find it helpful to organize your skeins of yarn onto swatch cards, which you can make yourself from strips of cardboard. Punch holes along the edges of the cardboard and loop the yarn through them. Mark the color number and name beside each one, and it will be an easy matter to find each color as you need it.

YOU WILL NEED

- **16 × 16in 10-gauge single canvas**
- **Paternayan Persian yarn, one skein each of:**

Red 971	812 Orange
Yellow 771	683 Green
Brown 881	300 Purple
Dark gray D389	D392 Pale gray
White 260	592 Turquoise
Pale turquoise 593	874 Flesh
	Black 220

- **Two skeins of:**

  Medium blue 554   555 Ice blue

- **Three skeins of:**

  Navy 571

- **Tapestry needle**
- **Acid-free mounting board**

KEY

Paternayan Persian yarn, as used in the Noah's Ark picture:

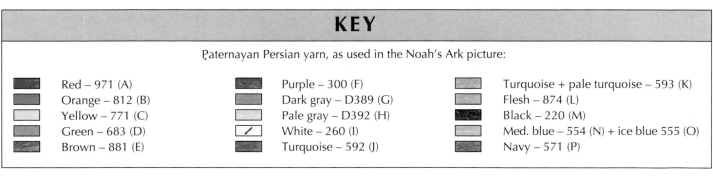

Red – 971 (A)
Orange – 812 (B)
Yellow – 771 (C)
Green – 683 (D)
Brown – 881 (E)

Purple – 300 (F)
Dark gray – D389 (G)
Pale gray – D392 (H)
White – 260 (I)
Turquoise – 592 (J)

Turquoise + pale turquoise – 593 (K)
Flesh – 874 (L)
Black – 220 (M)
Med. blue – 554 (N) + ice blue 555 (O)
Navy – 571 (P)

83

STITCH DETAILS

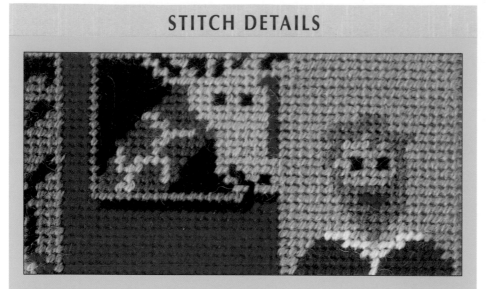

The bearded figure of Noah stands at the prow of the Ark, and the giraffe's head pokes through the window. The sky is worked in one strand each of medium blue and ice blue.

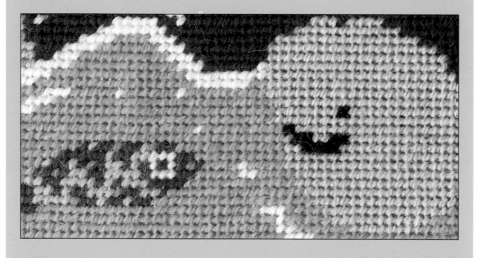

The fish has bright scales, and the friendly whale is pale gray. The two-tone effect on the sea is created by blending two shades of turquoise yarn in the needle.

The parrot perching on the roof of the Ark has plumage which echoes the colors of the rainbow beside it. The roof is worked in navy with green stripes.

Begin stitching the picture in the center. To secure the yarn at the beginning, leave a short length at the back of the canvas and work the first few stitches over it. To finish off, pass the needle under the last few stitches worked at the back and cut the end off short. Work the elephant first, using dark gray (D389) with black shading and white tusks. Then stitch the cabin of the Ark in red (971) and green (683) with a black interior.

Add the lion, the giraffe, and the snake as you come to them. Work in blocks of color, finishing one shade before starting the next, and remember not to take long strands across the back of the work from one part of the design to another. These may get caught up in subsequent stitching and will cause a lumpy effect on the front.

When you have finished the cabin, add the roof in navy (571) and green, stitching the butterfly and the parrot, too. Complete the hull of the Ark in navy with green and black portholes and a black band around the top. Work the monkey in brown (881), flesh (874), and black on the left-hand side and Noah himself on the right-hand side. His face is worked in flesh with black and red features, his hair and beard are dark gray, and his robe is purple (300) and white.

Complete the top part of the picture by filling in the sky with two shades of blue blended in the needle, using one strand each of medium blue (554) and ice blue (555). Add the rainbow and the dove. The sea is the finishing touch. Like the sky, this is worked in two different shades combined in the needle – this time, turquoise (592) and pale turquoise (593). The spray is white. The friendly-looking whale is stitched in pale gray (D392) with black features and a white water-spout. The fish are brightly colored in purple, yellow, (771) and green with white eyes.

FINISHING THE PICTURE

Remove the needlepoint from the frame. If it needs to be restored to shape, block it as described on pages 103–4. Cut the acid-free board to the size you require. The board illustrated measures 14¼ × 14¼ inches. Lace the needlepoint across the back of the board (see page 125). Alternatively, secure the raw edges at the back with masking tape. Mat and frame the finished picture as you wish. Choose a bright primary color for the frame to match one of the shades in the picture.

Ginger cat picture

This needlepoint marmalade cat surveys his
territory through a spacious window.

Ginger cat picture

YOU WILL NEED

- **4½ × 5¼in 16-gauge single canvas**
- **Paternayan Persian yarn, one skein each of:**

  Ginger 862   263 White

  Pale orange 885   850 Rust

  Yellow 710   612 Pale green

  Dark green 691   504 Blue

- **Tapestry needle**
- **Acid-free mounting board**

Cats are very individual creatures and are especially particular about the ownership of territory. When they are not surveying their patch of ground on foot, cats often choose to retire to the comfort of their home and look lazily out of the window. The pale and dark ginger markings on this cat look bold and striking against the rich greens of the garden.

STITCHING THE CAT

The chart is given on the right together with a key to the colors used. Each square on the chart represents one stitch in half cross-stitch on your canvas. The picture is worked on 16-gauge canvas using one strand of yarn.

Fold your piece of canvas in half each way and mark the center with lines of basting. Mark the center of the chart in pencil to correspond. Begin by stitching the background of the picture, so that you have a definite size to work within. The sky is worked in blue (504), and the trees and bushes are worked in two shades of green – pale green (612) and dark green (691). Next, work the bars of the window using white (263) and the windowsill underneath the cat in yellow (710). Finally, work the cat, using pale orange (885), ginger (862), and rust (850).

FINISHING

Finish the yarn ends on the back of your piece of canvas and mount the finished design on board, then frame it.

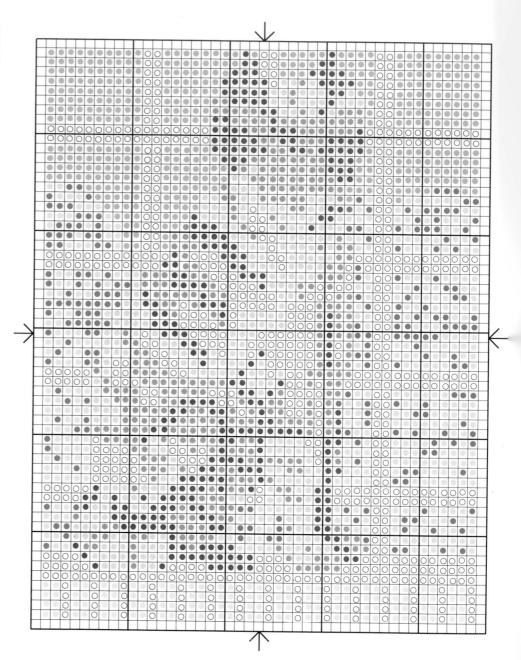

KEY

Paternayan Persian yarn, as used in the Ginger cat picture:

- Pale orange (885)
- Ginger (862)
- Rust (850)
- Yellow (710)
- Pale green (612)
- Dark green (691)
- Blue (504)
- ○ White (263)

Pen holder

Keep your best pens and pencils clean, scratch-free, and handy when you make this needlepoint holder.

Pen holder

*I*t is very annoying when someone asks you for a pen and you frantically search around for one with no success. With this pen holder, you can keep two pens, or a pen and pencil, together without having to carry around a large pencil case. The floral pattern makes this useful holder attractive and feminine and the finished design measures 1¾ × 5¼ inches.

WORKING THE DESIGN

Bind the edges of the canvas with masking tape. Fold your canvas in half each way and mark the central point with lines of basting. Begin working outward from the center of the chart on the left. Each dot on the chart represents one half cross-stitch, which is worked using one strand of Paternayan Persian yarn in the needle.

First work the vine and leaves, using dark green (521) for the shaded areas and pale green (D546) for the lighter parts. The flowers are worked in dark blue (502). You will find it easier to work one half, starting from the center, and then the other half. This means that the design can be placed correctly on the canvas. Next, work the maroon (900) stripes down each edge of the central pane. Work each side separately. Then work the background in pale yellow (713).

For the outer panels, first work the two dark blue vertical lines which will form their inner edge. The small flowers on the two outer panels are worked in pink (954) and maroon with dark green leaves. Finally, fill in the background in pale blue (564) and add the outer vertical lines in dark blue.

MAKING THE HOLDER

When you have finished stitching the design, gently stretch it back into a rectangular shape. If necessary, press carefully from the wrong side over a lightly padded surface. Trim loose ends carefully.

Place the needlepoint and the backing fabric together with right sides facing, and using sewing thread, backstitch around the side and bottom edges. Work close to the edge of the needlepoint stitches to prevent unworked canvas from showing through. Clip the lower corners to remove the excess fabric and then turn the holder right side out. Turn the raw edges of the canvas and then of the backing fabric under along the top and slipstitch them in position to form a long case.

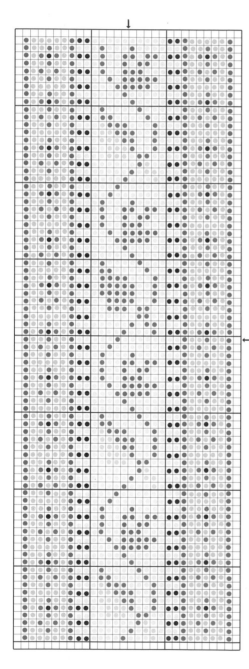

Follow the chart above to work the pen holder. Each colored dot equals one half cross-stitch and shows the correct color to use.

YOU WILL NEED

- **2¾ × 6in 16-gauge single canvas**
- **Paternayan Persian yarn, one skein each of:**

  Dark green 521   D546 Pale green
  Dark blue 502   900 Maroon
  Pink 954   713 Pale yellow
  Pale blue 564

- **Tapestry needle**
- **2¾ × 6in backing fabric**
- **Sewing needle and thread**

STITCH DETAILS

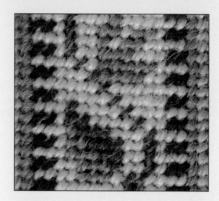

The center panel on the pen holder has pretty bell flowers and leaves on a pale yellow background.

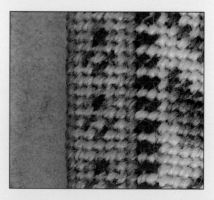

The two outer panels have small pink flowers on a pale blue background. A bright blue stripe edges the panel.

Dolphin pillow

Use this chart and key to work the border around the central design on the pillow. (The color chart for the central design is on page 24). Each square on the chart represents one stitch worked over one square of canvas.

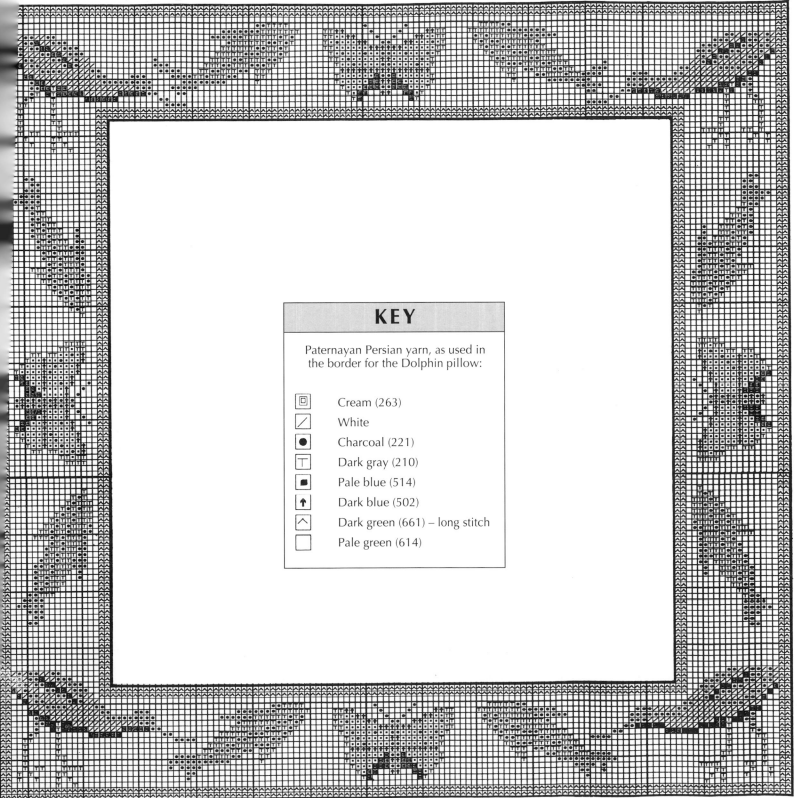

KEY

Paternayan Persian yarn, as used in the border for the Dolphin pillow:

▣	Cream (263)
╱	White
●	Charcoal (221)
⊤	Dark gray (210)
▪	Pale blue (514)
↑	Dark blue (502)
∧	Dark green (661) – long stitch
☐	Pale green (614)

Vine bolster

Use this chart and key (below and opposite) to work the needlepoint design for the bolster. Each square on the chart represents one stitch worked over one square of canvas.

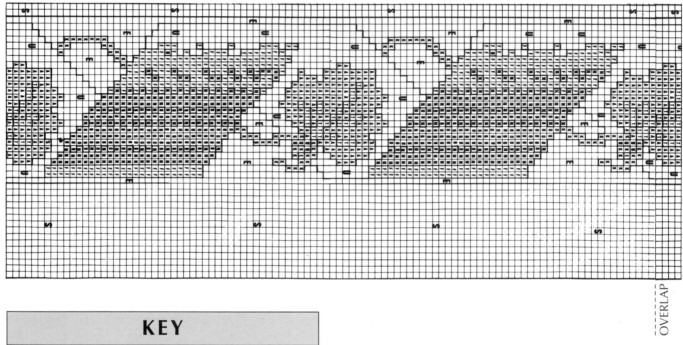

OVERLAP

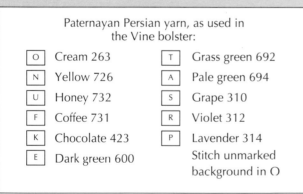

KEY

Paternayan Persian yarn, as used in
the Vine bolster:

O	Cream 263	T	Grass green 692
N	Yellow 726	A	Pale green 694
U	Honey 732	S	Grape 310
F	Coffee 731	R	Violet 312
K	Chocolate 423	P	Lavender 314
E	Dark green 600		Stitch unmarked background in O

The chart on this page is for the border panel worked on each side of the main panel; the chart opposite is for the main panel itself. Each chart shows a section of the whole design and should be repeated end to end.

To help you work the repeats, please refer to the pattern on page 92 which shows the full length of the design. Take care when matching each section of the design on eachr side of the "overlap" line. The design at the top of the canvas should match up with that at the bottom, so that the vine appears to wind continuously around the bolster. The border panel should run in the same direction on each side of the main panel, with the wide plain strip on the outside edge.

90

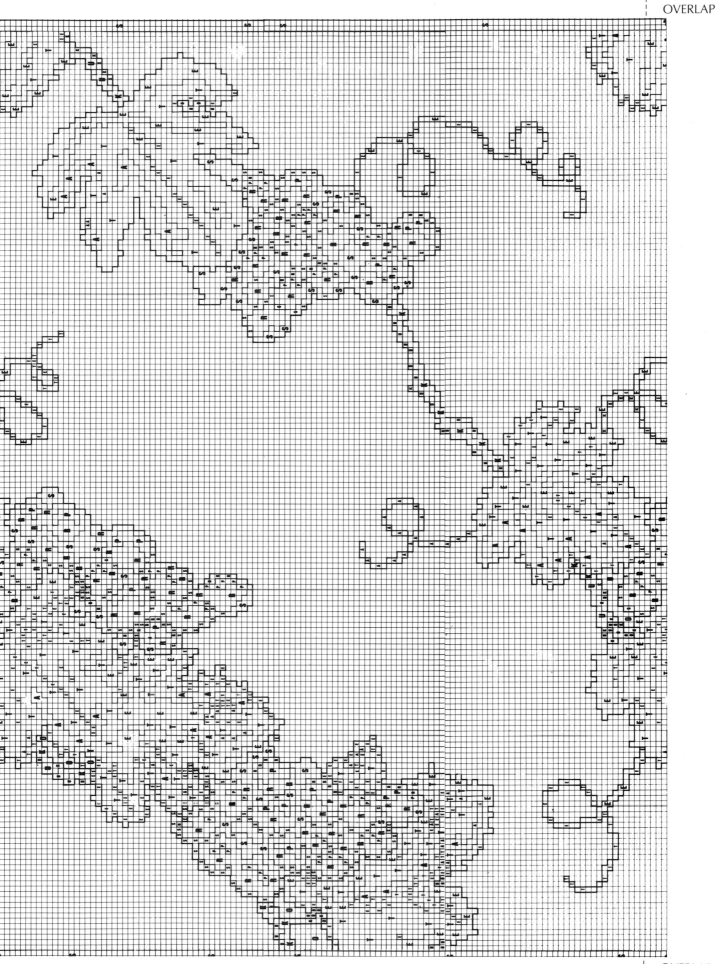

91

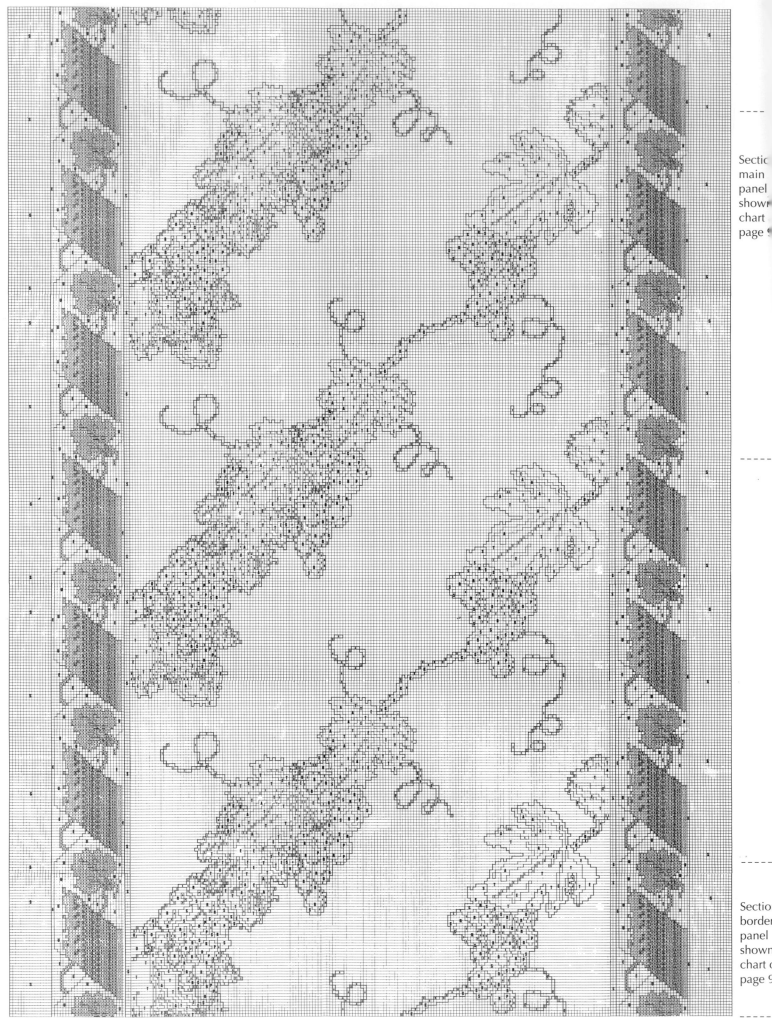

Section main panel shown chart page

Section of border panel shown on chart on page 90

Star pillow

This diagram shows one corner of the pillow. Use it as a guide to positioning the different needlepoint stitches used to work each square on the pillow. Follow the color key for each square given on the chart on page 28.

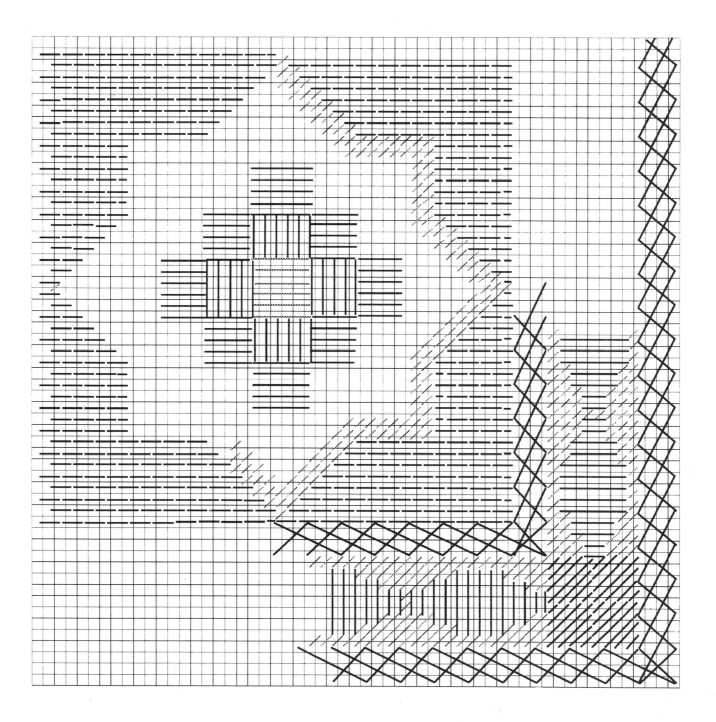

Spring picture

You will find it much easier to work the design if you transfer this outline onto your canvas and use it as a guide when stitching.
Using tracing paper and a pencil, trace around the outline, and transfer the design onto the canvas. Follow the color key given on the chart on page 58.

Tissue box cover

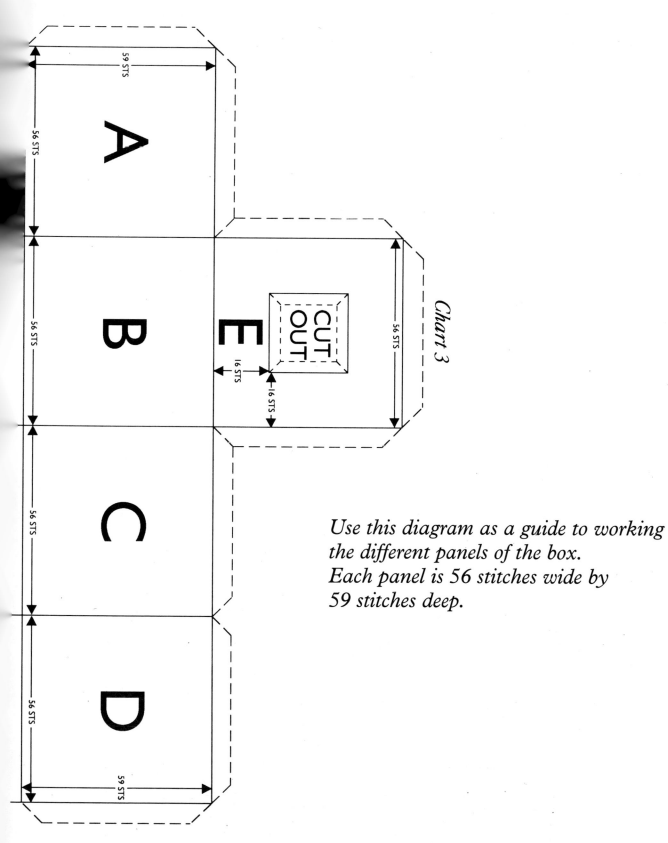

Chart 3

Use this diagram as a guide to working the different panels of the box.
Each panel is 56 stitches wide by 59 stitches deep.

Cat door-stop

Trace around the outlines below to make the pattern shapes for the bases of the cat and the weighted bag. Cut the base of the cat (A) from harmonizing backing fabric and the base of the weighted bag (B) from any plain cotton lining fabric.

(A)

(B)

Stitches and techniques

Introduction	98

BEFORE YOU START

Needles	99
Threads	101

FINISHING

Blocking canvas	103
Making pillow forms	105
Applying piping	107
Cords and braids	109

STITCHES

Continental stitch	111
Basketweave tent stitch	113
Long stitch	115
Gobelin stitches	117
Hungarian, Parisian, and brick stitches	119
Long-legged cross-stitch	121
Smyrna stitch	123
Half cross-stitch, split stitch, French knot, mounting canvas and scroll frame	125

Stitches and techniques

*A*lthough needlepoint is simple and straightforward, there are a few basics with which beginners and addicts alike need to be familiar. The following section outlines the fundamentals of stitching on canvas, as well as describing a few of the techniques that you might want to know about to help you complete the more intricate projects.

Both needles and yarns, essential for any needlepoint you might undertake, come in an array of sizes and types – and in the case of yarns, a huge variety of colors – that can be confusing to the newcomer. We take you through this maze briefly, but you will probably find that you want to explore the field more thoroughly on your own by visiting needlecraft shops and fairs to see for yourself the incredible range of yarn and types of canvas available.

Some of the projects in *The Needlepoint Collection* have been worked in stitches other than traditional tent stitch. Long stitch is a simple straight stitch that can be used horizontally or vertically very effectively. Long-legged cross-stitch is a variation on the more familiar cross-stitch and is a useful, quick background filling stitch.

The other section of this chapter provides information about assembling and finishing your completed needlepoint projects. The most beautifully stitched piece can be ruined by a poor finish, but all the techniques here are simple to do and will give a professional look to all your work. Making your own pillow forms, tassels, and cords and braids is not only much less expensive than buying ready-made ones, it also means your finished item will be "all of a piece," as you can use the same thread and fabric for finishing and match your colors exactly, and you can enjoy the satisfaction that goes with doing the whole job.

So don't worry about what to do with your completed needlepoint – just follow the clear step-by-step instructions in each section and you are on your way.

Needles

Needles are, of course, essential items of sewing equipment.
Stock your sewing box with a selection of different types,
and you'll always be sure of having just the right needle for each project.

For every stitching project, you need a needle – but what kind? There are so many different types and different sizes available that it's easy to become confused. Rest assured, however, that most of the rules for which needle you use for which type of embroidery are just common sense.

CHOOSING A NEEDLE

The size of your needle depends mainly on the size of your thread. The eye of the needle should be big enough to allow you to thread it easily, but small enough to hold the thread reasonably firmly once it is threaded. If the eye of your needle is too big, the thread will keep slipping out while you are sewing. The body of the needle should be just wide enough to pull the thread through your chosen fabric easily. If the needle is too fine, you will have to pull the thread through unnecessarily hard, which will affect the flow of your sewing and the tension of the stitches. If your needle is too large, you will make holes in the fabric that may not be hidden by the thread once it is pulled through.

The type of needle you use also depends on the kind of embroidery that you are doing. The two categories of needle are those with sharp tips and those with rounded or blunt tips. Sharp-tipped needles are used for most kinds of surface embroidery on ordinary closely woven fabrics and are available in several styles and many sizes to suit different threads and techniques.

Needles with rounded points, generally known as tapestry needles, are ideal for most needlepoint and cross-stitch. They are used for stitching on fabrics with noticeable holes, such as evenweave linen, aida fabric, binca cloth, and different types of canvas such as those used most often for needlepoint projects. Needles used on these fabrics do not need to pierce a hole to draw the thread through – in fact, a sharp tip is usually a drawback because it can split the threads and can spoil the look of the finished piece.

NEEDLE TYPES

Below are listed the most common types of needle you will come across when planning embroidery and craft projects.

Tapestry needles (A) have blunt tips; they are available in many sizes to suit every kind of evenweave fabric. They are the most suitable needles for use with needlepoint canvas.

Crewels (B) are the most frequently used embroidery needles; they are available in many sizes and have a large, long eye that is ideal for threads such as stranded floss, pearl cotton, and matte embroidery cotton.

Sharps (C) are fine needles with small eyes, useful for ordinary sewing thread, flower thread, and *coton à broder*. They are ideal for working hemming stitches and basting stitches on fine fabrics.

Betweens (D) are sharp needles which are slightly shorter than sharps and can be useful for fine quilting projects.

Quilting needles (E) come in many sizes; they are often long, so that you can take several stitches at one time with them.

Beading needles (F) are long and very fine so they will pass through the fine holes in small beads without breaking them.

Chenilles (G) are fairly large, sharp needles that have an extra-large eye to use with thick threads and yarns.

Rug needles (H) are like extra-large tapestry needles and are used for stitched rugs either on canvas or large-gauge binca.

Bodkins (I) are large, blunt needles which can be used for threading yarn and elastic through casings and ribbon through eyelets.

Blanket needles (J) are very strong semi-circular needles used in upholstery projects.

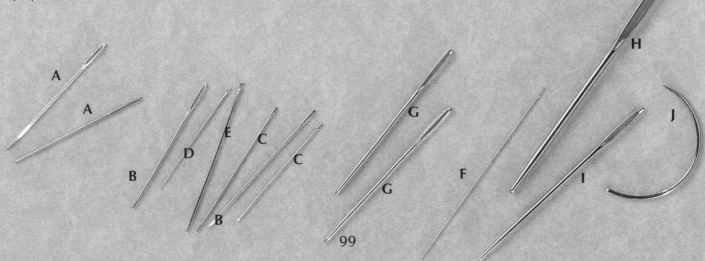

99

USING DIFFERENT NEEDLES

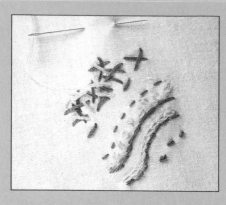

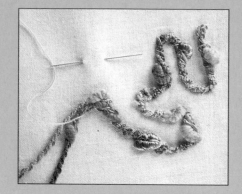

When you are embroidering in stranded floss or a similar thread on closely woven fabric, a **crewel needle** is usually the best needle to use.

For single threads which you are using for embroidery stitches or for couching down thicker threads, choose a fine **sharps, between,** or **crewel** needle.

Beading needles are especially long and fine so that they can pass through the tiny holes in small beads. For larger beads, use ordinary sharps and crewels.

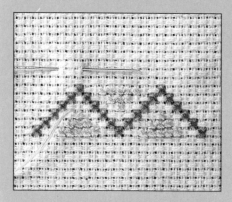

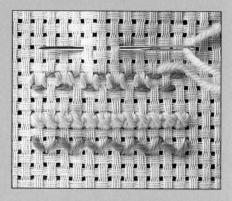

When you are working on fine evenweave fabric such as linen, hardanger or aida fabric, use a fine or medium **tapestry needle** that will not split the threads as you stitch.

Large-holed canvas needs to be worked with thicker threads and yarns to cover the background, so you will need a large-eyed **tapestry needle**.

If you are working on binca fabric or rug canvas which has very large holes, use a large tapestry needle or a special large-eyed **rug needle** which will be easy to thread.

WHAT WENT WRONG?

If the appearance of your embroidery does not seem quite right, you may discover that you have been using the wrong needle for the task.

In the first example, a crewel needle has been used instead of a blunt tapestry needle. The sharp tip has split the threads of the aida, producing uneven and unattractive cross-stitches.

In the second example, the needle is much too large for the background fabric and has a blunt tip instead of a sharp one. It has made large holes in the fabric, and the thread is too fine to fill and cover them.

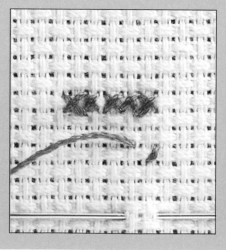

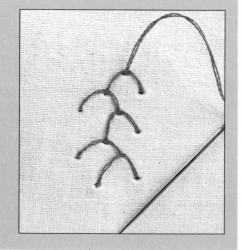

Threads

Any kind of thread can be used in embroidery, even ribbons, string, or strips of leather; but cotton, wool, and silk form the basis for nearly all classic stitching styles.

Your choice of thread is affected by many factors, both practical and artistic. Some embroidery or needlepoint stitches require a particular thread or yarn, and you should always try to use a thread which can be worked easily on your ground fabric.

In general, threads can be divided into two types: stranded and twisted. Twisted threads are made up of plies, which cannot be pulled apart, but stranded threads can be easily separated and recombined to give the thickness of thread you need. A ply is a single thread of spun yarn and, generally, the more plies, the thicker the yarn. Each of the three strands of yarn that make up the Persian yarn used in this book consists of two plies which cannot be separated.

COTTON

Different weights and types of cotton thread are suitable for surface embroidery and counted, drawn, and pulled-thread work. The strands of six-stranded embroidery floss are easily divided for fine work – or it can be used as it comes.

Soft embroidery cotton is a matte, medium-weight (5-ply), twisted thread, suitable for use on heavier fabrics, while pearl cotton (also called *perlé*) is somewhat finer. This 2-ply thread has a lustrous finish and is used in embroidery and also for smocking. It

is available in four different thicknesses: 3 (heavy), 5 (medium), 8 (fine), and 12 (very fine). *Coton à broder* is a twisted thread, finer than pearl cotton, but with similar uses. All three can be effective when used on needlepoint canvas.

WOOL

Crewel yarn is a 2-ply woolen yarn in which the single strand is slightly finer than one strand of Persian yarn. Unlike knitting yarns, crewel yarn does not fray easily when pulled through fabric, so it is used in embroidery on both heavy ordinary and evenweave fabrics in crewel work, and several strands thick for needlepoint.

Persian yarn is made up of three 2-ply strands and is the best choice for needlepoint on canvas, because you can vary the thickness to suit the gauge of the canvas. The same is not true of tapestry yarn, a thick 4-ply wool, which is slightly finer than three strands of Persian yarn.

OTHER THREADS

Use silk thread for fine work on fine fabric. Available in stranded and twisted forms, it gives a lovely finish, and the results more than justify the higher cost. Similarly, linen is sold as matte thread for smocking and counted thread work, and in its shiny form for cutwork and drawn thread work. Synthetic metallic threads are available in various weights, textures, and colors. They are ideal for highlighting or for small areas of solid stitching.

Clockwise from top right: fine silk in color-toned skeins, thick twisted silk, coton à broder, variegated cotton, and pearl cotton; two wool yarns in stranded and twisted forms, matte embroidery cotton, and metallic threads.

DIFFERENT EFFECTS WITH THREADS

Embroidery cotton – sold as coton à broder – a fine, twisted cotton available in different plies, suitable for delicate embroidery on fine fabrics. It is suitable for work only on fine canvas or evenweave fabrics.

Matte embroidery cotton – a soft, 5-ply twisted thread, ideal for work on medium- to loose-weave fabrics. Its thickness gives it good covering properties, making it suitable for fine needlepoint work, too.

Pearl cotton – a thick, twisted 2-ply cotton, this shiny thread gives an attractive finish with a slight sheen. Suitable for use on medium- to loose-weave fabrics and on fine needlepoint canvas.

Variegated cotton – a 2-ply pearlized cotton, thinner than regular pearl cotton, with subtle repeating changes of shade down its length. The shading produces delicate effects in finished embroidery.

Crewel yarn – a twisted yarn that is suitable as a single strand for use on medium- to loose-weave fabrics, or for needlepoint on canvas in several thicknesses, depending on the gauge of the canvas.

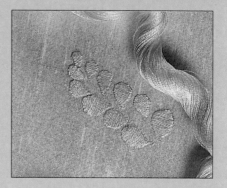

Silk – a fine, twisted 2-ply silk thread suitable for the finest embroidery on delicate fabrics. As it is so fine, it is sometimes easier to work with this silk using several thicknesses for better cover, as above.

Embroidery silk – this six-stranded thread can be used in any thickness to create satin-like effects. Although it is more expensive than cotton floss, the results are well worth the extra cost.

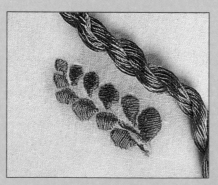

Metallic thread – available in various thicknesses and with different degrees of metallic content, these threads can be used alone or, in the case of very fine metallics, mixed with plain threads to give highlights.

Mixed silks – sold in hanks consisting of a bouclé thread, a thick soft thread, and strands of fine plain and variegated silk in harmonizing colors, these blends are effective when used on loose weaves and knits.

Blocking canvas

*Even the most painstakingly framed and stitched needlepoint
is likely to distort slightly in the making. Here is the tried and tested
method of getting any canvas back into shape.*

The process of stitching – especially diagonal stitching, as in tent stitch and half cross-stitch – tends to pull canvas out of shape. To restore it to symmetry, you will need to stretch and "block" the stitched work – the time this takes and the way in which you go about it will depend on how badly distorted the canvas is.

STITCHING FOR SHAPE

Keep distortion to a minimum by always having your canvas stretched in a scroll frame as you work. Also, when you stitch, keep the tension even and avoid tugging the yarn tightly – this, and using too thick a yarn, are the main causes of work in needlepoint taking on outlandish shapes.

The type of canvas has relatively little bearing on the way it distorts, as evenweave canvases are easier to block and stretch than interlocked ones – but the latter tend to hold their shape better anyway.

Measure the stitching area of your canvas, or calculate the size if you are working from a chart on plain canvas, and draw an outline on a sheet of thick, preferably graph, paper. You can use this as a guide to reshape the piece back to its original dimensions later.

SQUARING UP

Leave a good border – at least 1 to 2 inches – of canvas around the edge of your finished work, so that you have enough to get hold of when stretching and pinning it. Soften the work and make it more malleable by dampening it from the back. You can do this with a fine water spray, by wrapping it in a damp towel, or by dabbing it with a wet sponge. At this stage, if the work is only slightly distorted, all you need to do is stretch it gently by hand. For very distorted canvases, you need a completely plain, unpainted, unvarnished piece of

wood larger by at least 2 inches all around than the finished work and at least 1 inch thick – plywood is ideal. You can buy blocking boards marked in squares especially for this purpose; this is a good investment if you do a lot of needlepoint.

Pin or tape the outline of your stitched work to the board, as in the steps overleaf. If you like, pin it over a sheet of blotting paper for absorbency. Hold the work firmly by the canvas edges and pull steadily against the distortion, then place the work on the board, pinning to the outline using thumbtacks no more than 1¼ inches apart. Put them in the unworked canvas so as not to pull the stitch-

ing, and keep stretching the canvas gently into shape as you work around it. Adjust the thumbtacks more as the canvas starts to give. A badly distorted piece may need additional dampening and pinning before it can be squared up. Once you have the shape you want, leave the canvas on the board to dry in a warm, well-ventilated place, away from direct light and heat. Do not be tempted to take it off the board until it is completely dry.

Even a badly distorted canvas can be coaxed back into symmetrical shape with the help of thumbtacks and a wooden board.

HOW TO BLOCK A CANVAS

1 *This design, worked in continental tent stitch, should be square, but it has been pulled out of shape by the diagonal slant of the stitching. The distortion might have been less had the work been kept taut in a frame.*

2 *Draw an outline of the work as it should be on graph paper and mark the center of each side, using a pencil or waterproof pen. Pin the graph paper to a plywood or other type of thick wooden board.*

3 *Dampen the stitched canvas thoroughly by sponging it from the back with warm water (as above) or by using a fine spray on the back, or by rolling the canvas in a wet white or colorfast towel.*

4 *Grip the damp canvas firmly by the unstitched edges and pull steadily against the distortion to get the canvas into a better shape before you start to block it on the prepared wooden board.*

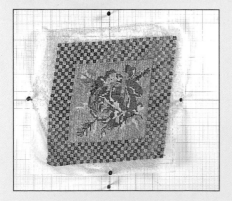

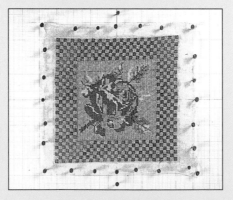

5 *Pin the canvas over the outline on the board, matching the center of each side to the marked points. Pin the corners to match the shape with thumbtacks 1¼in apart.*

6 *Use a carpenter's square or the corner of a magazine to check that each corner is a right angle. Restretch if necessary. Allow the canvas to dry completely before removing it.*

MILD DISTORTION

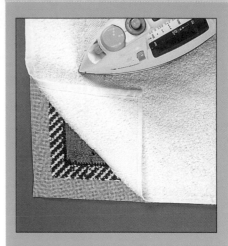

If your canvas is only slightly distorted, you might not need to go through the full stretching and blocking process. Often, all you need to do is press the canvas from the back using a steam iron; then pull the canvas firmly back into shape by hand. If this is not enough, dampen the canvas further by placing a damp towel between the iron and the canvas, and then pin the work out as in the steps on the left. Always make sure the stitching has dried completely before you unpin it from the board or it may start to contract.

BLOCKING MACHINE

An investment for enthusiastic needle-pointers, the blocking machine shown above does the work for you. As they are relatively expensive to buy, they are probably not worth the cost for the occasional stitcher – you might like to try a blocking service offered by some companies as advertized in needlework and craft magazines instead.

Making pillow forms

One of the secrets of successful pillow-making is having the right pillow form. Here we show how to make your own.

Feather

If you want a pad for an unusual shape or size of pillow or just want to economize, it is useful to know how to make your own. Making pillow forms is straightforward; the steps are logical and can easily be adapted for different shapes and sizes.

FABRICS FOR PILLOW FORMS

The best fabrics to use are firmly woven cottons. They are easy to work with, keep their shape well without distorting under the pressure of the stuffing, and are cheap and readily available. It is best to choose white or cream, in case your pillow cover is thin and the pad shows through, though if you are making pads especially for dark pillow covers, you can use leftovers of dark cotton fabric.

Firmly woven cambric, cotton sheeting, or similar fabrics are very good and usually cheap. Chintz and polished cotton can be used, but are more expensive. Many people use muslin, which is cheap. The sizing that is used on some cotton fabrics, including muslin, as well as the firm weave, help the fabric – and therefore the pillow form – to keep its shape. If you are using feathers or down as a stuffing, it is worth paying more for down-proof cotton. If you don't, the feathers may work their way through the fabric.

STUFFINGS FOR PILLOW FORMS

Many materials are available as filling for pillow forms. Your choice will probably depend on the size and type of the pillow, the desired texture of the finished pillow, and how much money you want to spend.

The most expensive stuffing is **feathers**, or a mixture of feathers and down. Down is the extra-fluffy feather-like material that grows under a bird's main feathers. Feathers and down give a smooth, satisfactory finish with just the right amount of squash or give.

Foam chips are cheap and readily available. They give a springy feel and can be quite hard if the pillow is firmly stuffed. The smaller the chips, the better, but avoid cheap versions full of big, firm lumps. Also, make sure that any foam you use is flame-retardant.

Styrofoam balls are ideal for large floor pillows or items for which you need a filling that moves around to take on the required shape. These, too, are cheap, but they can give off noxious fumes if they catch fire. Also, they do eventually compress, so you will have to top up the pillow filling after a while.

Other stuffings include **kapok**, a natural stuffing which is soft but which can tend to flatten or go into lumps, and **synthetic filling**, which is washable.

When making your own pillow forms, bear in mind the safety aspect of the materials you plan to use. Whenever possible, choose flame-retardant fabrics and fillings. Also bear in mind that most needlepoint pillows will not be easily washable and choose a stuffing that can be dry-cleaned if possible.

Down

Foam chips

Styrofoam balls

Kapok

Synthetic filling

HOW TO MAKE A SQUARE PILLOW FORM

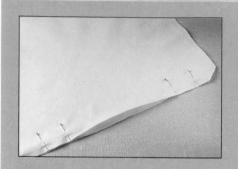

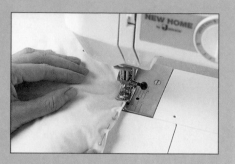

1 Cut two squares of fabric the size you want your finished pillow form to be plus seam allowances. Stitch along the seam line, leaving several inches open in one side.

2 Clip the corners, turn right side out, and press. Fill with stuffing through the gap; don't over-stuff, or the pillow will be too firm.

3 Fold under the raw edges around the gap; pin them together, then stitch neatly close to the outside of the fabric to close the opening.

HOW TO MAKE A CIRCULAR PILLOW FORM WITH A GUSSET

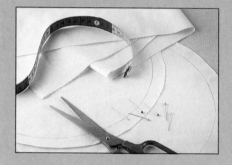

1 Cut two circles the size of your pad plus seam allowances. Measure the circumference. Cut a gusset to this length by the required depth, plus seam allowances.

2 To make the gusset, stitch the ends of the fabric strip to form a circle, then pin, baste, and stitch around one circle, right sides together, easing the fabric around the curve.

3 Attach the gusset to the other circle in the same way, leaving a gap for stuffing. Trim the seams, then turn, fill, and close by hand or machine-stitching.

bright idea

For a scented or herbal pillow, put some potpourri or fragrant dried herbs inside the pillow form. Mix them with some stuffing as well; otherwise, the pillow will be hard and lumpy.

WHAT WENT WRONG?

It is important to put in just the right amount of stuffing. The aqua pillow has been filled with a form that is too big and too firmly stuffed; the shape is distorted, and the pillow has no squash or give. The plaid pillow has a pad that is too small and flat; it has lost all its shape and cannot provide any support.

Applying piping

Piping in a matching or contrasting fabric sets off all manner of pillows and upholstery to perfection. Here's how to achieve a professional finish.

To show any type of pillow off to look its very best, trim it with corded piping in a color and fabric of your choice. It is not at all difficult, and it gives a very neat, professional edge. A variety of effects can be achieved by using piping in a color complementary to the pillow, in a contrasting color, or one of a different texture.

MAKING PIPING

Although it is possible to buy ready-made piping in standard colors, or braid specially set on a strip which can be applied like piping, making your own is very easy.

When you are buying piping cord, you will first need to measure the edges of the pillow which you wish to trim and allow at least 4 inches for turning and fraying. If you intend to wash the finished pillow cover, it is a good idea to wash the piping cord itself before you apply it in case it shrinks.

Select a gauge of cord which will suit the weight of the fabric and size of the pillow. Now you can choose whether you want to use ready-made bias binding or cut bias strips in a fabric to match your pillow.

For bias binding simply buy the same length as the piping cord, in a width that will leave you at least a 1-inch seam allowance when it is doubled over the cord. Bias-cut fabric stretches around corners, so it is ideal for this kind of trimming, but if you want to make your own binding from a piece of your chosen material, you will need to cut your own bias strips of fabric.

CUTTING BINDING

First lay out your fabric as shown in the steps overleaf and fold the horizontal grain of one end up to lie along the vertical grain. Press the fabric along this fold with a warm iron and then cut along the fold. Now all you need to do is cut strips of the required width, keeping them parallel to the first cut. Cut a width which will leave 1 inch of doubled fabric free when folded over the cord.

To trim a pillow, you will need to join several strips – do this following step 3 (over) to make a continuous strip. Press the turned seam so it lies flat, and trim the edges evenly.

To make the piping itself, fold the binding in half along its length, wrong sides together, enclosing the cord. Pin and baste firmly so that the stitching is right next to the length of piping cord.

APPLYING THE PIPING

Lay out the fabric for the pillow front, right side up, and mark a 1-inch seam allowance all around. Take the piping and, starting in the center of one side, pin the piping along the seam line, the cord lying just inside the seam-line, carefully shaping it around the corners.

When you come to join the two ends of piping in the seam, cut the cord inside the two pieces to abut exactly and cut the binding on one end even with the cord. Trim the binding on the other end to within 1¼ inches of the end of the piping and fold under a 1-inch hem. Pull this end over the other end of the piping to cover it like a sleeve; then, making sure it is lying flat, pin and baste it in place all around.

Stitch the piping in place, either by hand in backstitch, or by machine using a zipper or piping foot to keep the stitching close to the piping cord. Snip the corners of the binding so they lie flat at the corners. Place the back of the pillow over the front, right sides together. Pin and baste in place around three sides and stitch over the previous line of stitching.

Fill the pillow with a suitable pad, then fold back a 1-inch allowance down the edge of the backing, and fold in the piped edge along the line of the stitching. Pin the two together and baste in place, then slipstitch together to complete the pillow.

Choose a fabric to complement the color of the pillow for a really professional finish.

HOW TO MAKE PIPING

1 Mark the horizontal straight grain of the piping fabric and fold it up to meet the vertical grain. Press this diagonal fold to form a sharp crease, then cut along the fold to make one edge of the bias binding.

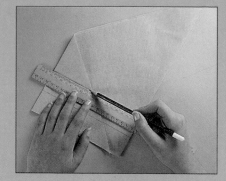

2 Depending on the thickness of your piping cord, mark lines an appropriate width from the diagonal you have cut, keeping them parallel. Cut strips to give the length of binding you need.

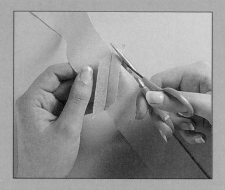

3 To join two strips of binding, place two ends right sides together so that they form a right angle. Make a 1-in seam, then press it open so that the binding forms a continuous strip. Snip off the triangle edges.

4 Take the piping cord (washed if necessary to prevent shrinkage) and lay along the center of the wrong side of the binding. Fold to enclose piping cord, matching the edges, and pin and baste next to the cord.

5 Press the fabric for the pillow front and mark a 1-in seamline all around it. Pin the piping to the right side of the fabric, matching the basted line to the seamline and curving the piping at the corners.

6 Where piping ends meet, cut the cord to abut and trim one end of binding even with its cord. Leave a 1¼-in overlap of binding on the other end, press in a 1-in hem, and pull it over the short end. Pin in place.

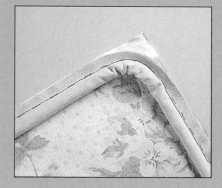

7 Stitch the piping to the pillow front either by hand using backstitch or by machine using a piping foot to keep the stitching close to the piping cord all the way around.

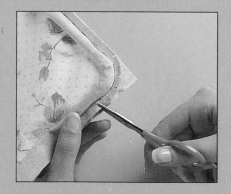

8 At the corners, snip the binding to within a couple of threads of the stitching so that it fans out and lies evenly against the pillow front. Press and mark a seam allowance on the pillow back.

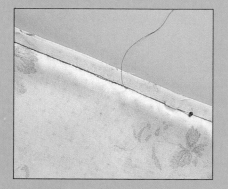

9 Attach the back to the front on three sides, right sides together, pinning along the stitching and keeping the cord inside the seam. Turn right side out, insert pad; turn in open edges and slipstitch.

Cords and braids

Making your own cords and braids is surprisingly easy, and they can be used to add the perfect finishing touch to all kinds of projects, from pillow covers to accessories and garments.

Cords and braids have many uses to the needleworker. You can make fine or textured versions and incorporate them into needlepoint and embroidery projects, or use thicker cords for couching down with stitches in a contrasting thread. Or you may find that you want an edging for a piece of embroidery, such as a throw pillow or footstool cover. For all these different uses, it is very satisfying to make just the kind of cord or braid you want, in exactly the right thickness, using the perfect colors of thread.

WHAT ARE CORDS AND BRAIDS?

Cords are simply twisted hanks of thread. The mistake that many people make when they are making their own cords is to use only a single twist of thread. Stable cords, which do not unravel easily, are formed from double twists, where the batch of threads has been twisted tightly and then allowed to double back on itself. It is much easier to use a cord for your projects when it is not trying to unravel all the time.

Braids are plaits of threads. The traditional braid is made from three hanks of threads plaited together, and this is the easiest kind to make if you are a beginner, but if you are good at plaiting, you will know that more than three hanks can be plaited at the same time. The principle is the same, but using more hanks takes a little practice and is best done on a flat surface such as a macramé board so that you can see where you are. If you use hanks of different colors, you will be able to see very easily whether you have kept the hanks in the right order as you plait.

MATERIALS TO USE

Both cords and braids can be made using the same thread throughout, or using a mixture of many different threads. You can make both cords and braids with any kind of thread, from the finest silk to the thickest yarn, but remember that some threads are so fine that you will need many lengths to make a braid or cord of a significant thickness.

If you want a very fine cord or braid, you will need to use a very fine thread to make it, or use just a few strands of a coarser thread. So, for instance, for a fine cord to edge a silk-covered box, you could twist quite a large number of strands of silk thread, which is very delicate and twists very tightly, or just a few strands of a thicker thread such as pearl cotton. If you want a thick cord, you could use many strands of fine thread such as floss, or just a few strands of a thick wool yarn. Remember, though, that if you are making a cord, the final cord will be twice the thickness that you see when you have made the preliminary twist, because you allow it to double back on itself.

Both cords and braids look very effective made in a selection of threads of different colors and textures. If you are making an edging for a particular project, try to use the leftover threads from the project itself, blending the colors so that they reflect the color mix in the piece of work. If you are making something for a subtle piece of work, blend the colors of your cord or braid subtlely; similarly, if you are making an edging for a bright, bold piece, be more adventurous with the color choice for your cords and braids.

The cords and braids shown here can be home-made, using threads varying from thick, matte cottons to fine metallics. These examples demonstrate well the different effects you can achieve by varying the colors, textures, and thicknesses of threads.

HOW TO MAKE A FINGER BRAID

1 Wind a hank of thread twice the required length of the braid. Cut the looped edges at the bottom. Secure the top to a solid object such as a chair back, or with a thumbtack.

2 Divide the large hank into three equal hanks of thread and begin plaiting them, taking the hank from each side in turn and weaving it over and under the others.

3 When you have plaited the whole length of the threads, secure the end with a knot so that the braid cannot unravel. The braid is now ready for you to use.

HOW TO MAKE A FINGER CORD

1 Cut lengths of thread three times the required length of the cord. Knot the ends. Tie or hook the top around something solid, or pin it securely to a wooden surface.

2 Using a pencil, keep the hank taut and twist the threads steadily in one direction until you have twisted the whole hank firmly. Bring the end of the hank up to the top.

3 If you have made the preliminary twist firm enough but not too tight, the two halves of the cord will twist smoothly and securely together and will not unravel.

bright ideas

There are endless threads and yarns that can be used to create unusual cords and braids. In these two examples, knitting yarns have been used to create textured effects.

The upper example is a plaited finger braid which has been made from three fancy knitting yarns of the same weight.

In the lower example, a mohair knitting yarn and a smooth ribbon yarn have been combined to make a twisted finger cord. This has been loosely wound to make the most of the sheen on the ribbon yarn.

WHAT WENT WRONG?

Your cord will not work properly if it is twisted too tightly. In the example shown here, the cord has been over-wound so that it has become distorted and irregular instead of forming a neat, double twist.

Continental tent stitch

Easy to learn and quick to do, tent stitch is a frequently used needlepoint stitch. It is also one of the most hard-wearing, which makes it particularly useful for pillows and upholstery.

Tent stitch, also known as "petit point," is perhaps the most useful needlepoint stitch you will ever learn. A small diagonal stitch, tent stitch gives a smooth, flat surface which is ideal for creating pictures in yarn on canvas, or forming a smooth background for other heavier, more textured needlepoint stitches.

SUPER STITCH

Continental tent stitch is the most versatile form of tent stitch. It can be worked in horizontal or vertical rows, or diagonally across the canvas. You will find it a particularly useful stitch for portraying intricate detail on canvas, or outlining a motif.

When working this form of tent stitch, there is a danger that the canvas will become pulled out of shape. To counteract this, try to maintain an even tension at all times. To further avoid stretching the canvas out of shape, it is always advisable to work on a scroll frame (see page 125).

A GOOD BEGINNING

If you have never worked tent stitch, practice on a scrap of canvas before embarking on a project. Use single canvas and a loosely twisted yarn. Thread your needle with enough strands of yarn to cover the canvas adequately, but not so many that it will be difficult to pull the yarn through the holes, as this will produce a bulky, untidy effect.

Do not use too long a thread when stitching, as it will wear and break with the friction of being pulled through the canvas; 18 inches is a good length. The thread will twist during stitching, so let the needle hang loose every so often. Work your way methodically across the canvas as far as possible, rather than darting about, doing a few stitches here and there. The back of your work should be almost as neat as the front! Avoid straggly ends by clipping off all secured threads as you go.

GUIDE TO CANVAS

Needlepoint canvas can be made of linen, plastic, paper, even silk, but the most popular material is cotton. Single canvas is made up of single vertical and horizontal threads. Double canvas is formed by the interweaving of parallel pairs of threads. Choose double canvas if your design is a complex one and is likely to include both large and small stitches.

There are two types of single and double canvas: evenweave, also known as plain, and interlock. The threads of evenweave canvas are not joined to each other, whereas the threads of interlock canvas are fused together at the points where they intersect. Evenweave canvas is best for upholstery and pillows because the threads are less likely to snap. Interlock canvas, however, does not become as distorted as evenweave canvas.

CONTINENTAL TENT STITCH

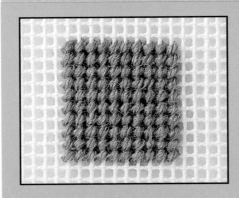

FRONT   The smooth texture of tent stitch as shown here can only be produced if the tension is even, and the yarn is not pulled too tightly or allowed to be too slack.

BACK   When you are working continental tent stitch, the back of your canvas should be covered by long diagonal stitches, each one crossing two vertical canvas threads.

111

HOW TO WORK CONTINENTAL TENT STITCH

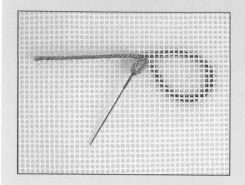

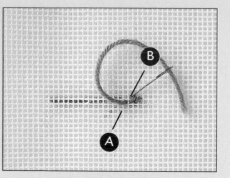

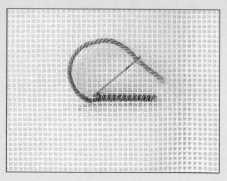

1 *(Back of work) Start by taking the needle through to the canvas front, passing it across one intersection and bringing it out again, leaving a yarn end of 1½–2in.*

2 *To work a stitch, bring the needle out at A, take it over one intersection, insert it at B, pass it under two vertical threads, and bring it out through the hole next to A.*

3 *Work in this way from right to left across the canvas. Use a stabbing motion, taking the needle right through to the canvas back before returning to the front again.*

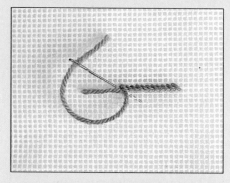

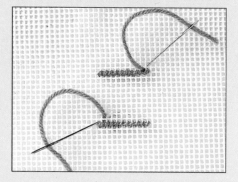

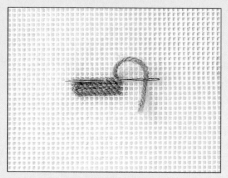

4 *(Back of work) As you work, hold the yarn end against the canvas, so the first few stitches bind it in place. Trim off the remaining loose end and continue stitching.*

5 *Working from right to left, start a new row as shown (top) and continue. To start a new row working from left to right, move upward as shown (bottom).*

6 *(Back of work) To finish, weave the yarn through a few stitches, then snip off the end. Never knot yarn ends. Wherever possible, start new lengths of yarn in the same way.*

CONTINENTAL TENT STITCH WORKED VERTICALLY AND DIAGONALLY

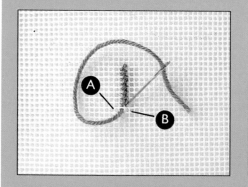

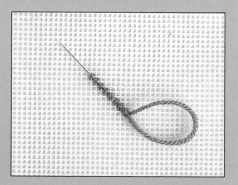

VERTICAL To work a stitch in a vertical line, bring the yarn up at A, insert the needle at B, take the yarn under two horizontal threads and bring it up again one hole below A, ready to begin the next stitch.

LEFT DIAGONAL When you work a diagonal row down to the left, the stitches form a straight line – ideal for outlining. To form each stitch, take the needle diagonally under two vertical thread intersections.

RIGHT DIAGONAL A diagonal row down to the right produces a saw-toothed edge – the stitches do not touch. They can be visually linked by a line of yarn threaded under the completed row of stitches.

Basketweave tent stitch

Popular with needleworkers since the earliest beginnings of needlepoint, this tent stitch variation remains one of the most versatile and durable of all canvas stitches. Use it for all types of upholstery for a really hard-wearing result.

Like the continental variety, basketweave tent stitch is a small, diagonal stitch which is worked on canvas. Both types of tent stitch are worked in rows, but the difference between the two is that continental tent stitch is worked horizontally or vertically and basketweave is worked diagonally. Although the two types of tent stitch look identical on the front of the work, the effect on the back of the canvas is very different. Basketweave tent stitch produces a distinctive interlocking or "basketweave" effect – hence its name. The two stitches use about the same amount of yarn but basketweave covers both sides of the canvas and produces therefore a very durable result. Most of the early needlepoint pieces which have survived through the centuries were worked in basketweave tent stitch, which shows how hard-wearing it is.

READING THE CANVAS

When working basketweave tent stitch on evenweave canvas, it is important to "read" the grain of the canvas for the best results. If you look closely at the canvas, you will see that at one intersection the vertical thread is on top and at the next the horizontal thread is on top. On a diagonal line of intersections, the top threads will all be either vertical or horizontal, alternating on each diagonal. The simple rule is: work rows down over vertical top threads and rows up over horizontal top threads.

Apart from producing a really smooth result, there are several advantages to reading the grain of the canvas. When you are working on very fine canvas,

you will prevent the stitches from disappearing between the threads of the canvas when they are worked in the wrong direction. Also you can work in different areas of the canvas and when you fill in the background, you will not get unsightly diagonal ridges where two adjacent rows are worked in the same direction. With some practice, you will soon be able to tell whether the next row to be worked should go up or down when you pick up a partially worked piece of canvas.

STITCHING IN ROWS

If you have never worked basketweave tent stitch before, it is best to practice on a piece of scrap canvas first before embarking on a needlepoint project. The short rows and the constant changing of direction can be confusing to a beginner, and it is easy to skip stitches at the ends of the rows. Be careful not to make a half cross-stitch at the edges instead of a tent stitch – half cross-stitch covers the back of the canvas with very little yarn and is less hard-wearing. If you find changing direction difficult at the end of each row, remember to rotate the needle one hole toward the center of the design before you continue.

Basketweave tent stitch works best when used to fill in backgrounds or large areas of color as it does not distort the canvas and wears extremely well.

HOW TO WORK BASKETWEAVE TENT STITCH

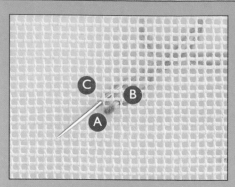

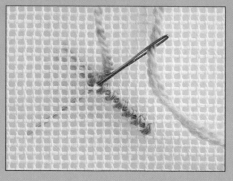

1 *Working diagonally, bring the needle out at A, take it up to the right over one intersection, and insert it at B. Take the needle across two vertical threads and bring it out at C.*

2 *Continue working stitches up to the left in a diagonal line up to the end of the row. Work stitches over loose yarn at back of work while holding it in place with your finger.*

3 *To start the next row, take needle up across two vertical threads at the back and bring it out ready to form the next stitch. Continue as before, filling spaces left from previous row.*

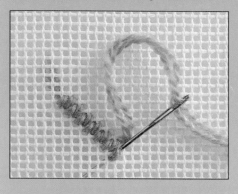

4 *To begin a third row, change direction by taking the needle up one horizontal thread and across two vertical threads at the back. Work in a diagonal row up to the left.*

5 *At the end of the third row, change direction as in step 3 to go diagonally down to the right again. Keep the edge of each new row in line with previously worked rows.*

6 *(Back of work) Secure the end of the yarn by passing the needle under a few stitches on the back. The rows of worked stitches form a distinctive basketweave pattern.*

BASKETWEAVE TENT STITCH AS A FILLING STITCH

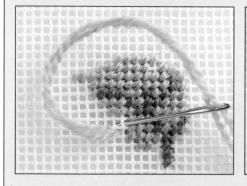

Work diagonally wherever possible to fill in areas of solid background color. Once you have stitched the details of a design horizontally in continental tent stitch, fill in around the shapes using basketweave tent stitch.

Work basketweave tent stitch diagonally and continue in rows as explained in the steps above. This is the quickest and simplest way to fill in large areas of canvas. On the front of the work, the two types of stitches look identical.

On the back of the work, the difference between the rows of continental tent stitch (green) and the basketweave pattern (pink) is clear. Although worked differently, the two varieties use about the same amount of yarn.

Long stitch

One of the simplest of all needlepoint stitches, long stitch can be used to create textures, patterns, and shading – and it is remarkably quick to cover canvas, too.

The special feature of long stitch is that it is worked vertically or horizontally, but the stitches never cross the canvas threads diagonally – and you do not have to stitch into every hole, as with tent stitch. This makes it a very speedy stitch to work in, covering large areas quickly.

USING LONG STITCH

This quick "filling" quality makes long stitch very popular for creating needlepoint pictures – its versatile length makes it ideal for subtle shading or texturing within a single color area. Long stitch lends itself very well to geometric patterns, too, so it can be used to great effect in soft furnishings and upholstery. Because the stitch covers the back of the canvas, it has hard-wearing qualities, too.

STITCH COVERAGE

Always use enough strands of yarn or embroidery thread for the gauge of your canvas. On a large gauge, such as 10-count, you will need all three strands of Paternayan Persian yarn, but you can reduce this for a smaller-gauge canvas. If in doubt, try a small area of stitching on a corner of the canvas to check the cover.

It is also important not to make the stitches too long – anything over 1 inch will need to be worked in two stitches. (See How to work long stitch overleaf). With this technique, you can add textured detail to your stitching and avoid leaving long, loopy stitches.

TEXTURES AND SHADES

Using rows of abutting stitches, you can create random or geometric texturing, working each subsequent row of stitches to share the holes in which the previous row was worked. When you have completed one row of stitches, start the second row below the base of the last stitch in the first row, taking the needle back down into the bottom of the existing stitch (see steps overleaf).

Long stitch is a stabbing stitch, so you must complete one movement of the thread before bringing the needle through the canvas again. This reduces wear on the yarn or thread and also helps to keep the canvas in shape. Make sure you keep the tension even – this is especially important on longer stitches. The shape of the finished work will be better if you keep the canvas stretched in a frame – this will also help you keep an even tension throughout.

VERTICAL AND HORIZONTAL

Different textures can be achieved by using a mixture of vertical and horizontal stitching for different colored areas. For details of how to abut stitching, see steps overleaf.

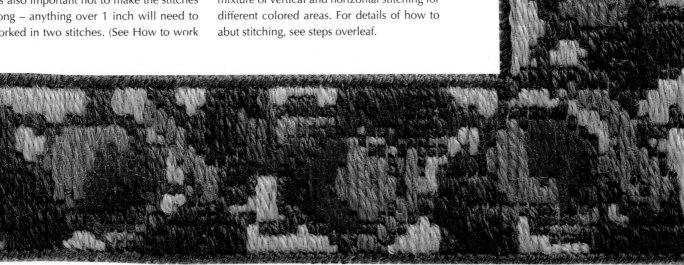

HOW TO WORK LONG STITCH

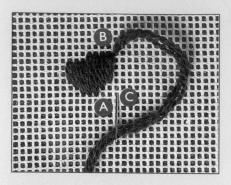

1 *Working over the thread at the back of the canvas as you go, bring needle behind the canvas from A to come up at B, then stitch down into C, directly below B to make the next stitch.*

2 *BACK The reverse of a piece of long stitch shows the canvas completely covered, with the threads making a slightly diagonal pattern. This back and front coverage makes long stitch hard-wearing.*

3 *To avoid long stitches, break up large areas in a straight or uneven line. Complete a row of stitching; bring the thread up below the row of stitches and stitch into the shared hole immediately above.*

HOW TO WORK GEOMETRIC LONG STITCH

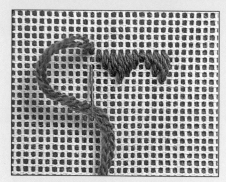

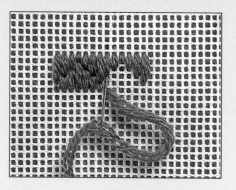

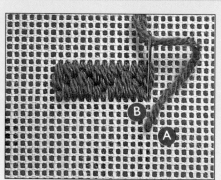

1 *To make a geometric pattern, take each successive stitch on the top row one thread lower down the canvas up to five threads, then continue taking each stitch over one less thread of canvas.*

2 *In the next row, work so the bottom of each stitch forms a line, working each stitch into a shared hole from the row before. Bring the needle up below the last stitch, mirroring a short stitch with a long one, and so on.*

3 *Always work down into a hole shared with another stitch, B, and bring the needle up in an empty hole, A. This ensures that loose fibers dragged by the movement of the needle are taken under the canvas, not on the top.*

DIFFERENT EFFECTS WITH COLOR

1 *Use different shades of the same color in random stitching, as in the interlocking rows of long stitch (far left). The effect is of a smooth satin stitch with subtle variations in color.*

2 *You can use long stitch horizontally and vertically together to contrast colors and textures. Be sure when stitching at a right angle to existing stitching that you finish stitches in the holes just covered by the abutting stitch.*

116

Gobelin stitches

The slightly slanting Gobelin stitches, named after the famous Parisian tapestry workshops, can be used to give your needlepoint projects the even appearance and texture of woven tapestry.

The original Gobelin workshop, founded in Paris in 1662 as a royal factory to supply furnishings for the French crown was the first true school of tapestry weaving in the world. The weavers had a long six-year apprenticeship; then they had to work in the workshops for a further period of four years before they had the right to set up independently. The most experienced craftsmen were known as the *officiers de tête*. These were the only weavers who were considered skilled enough to work on the faces and other flesh areas of figures, as these required the most subtle shading.

The beautiful and realistic tapestries produced by the Gobelin workshop gradually became known throughout the world and encouraged the setting up of many imitators of the original school. This spread of knowledge and skill all helped to make the craft of tapestry weaving more popular and better appreciated as it gained recognition.

SUBTLE SHADING

In particular, the craftsmen in the Gobelin workshop soon developed a reputation for the neatness and regularity of their weaving. Originally, they used between 15 and 18 warp threads per inch; then, during later centuries, they began working with between 18 and 20 warp threads per inch; this greater number of threads, combined with the

incredible 30,000 shades of yarn dyed in the Gobelin dye works, allowed an astonishing subtlety of color shading that was just as realistic as painting.

TAPESTRY-LIKE STITCHES

For many years, needlepoint was known as tapestry work, probably because the even texture of the stitching was similar to that found in fine tapestries. This may be the reason that the long, even stitches shown here were named "Gobelin stitches" – they produce a very regular effect in horizontal lines, giving the effect of the surface of woven tapestry.

Some Gobelin stitches are worked straight up and down, making them very similar to long stitch or brick stitch, but the versions shown here are all worked at a gentle slant, which allows the basic stitch to be interlocked and plaited. Basic Gobelin stitch is similar to tent stitch, but is worked at a slight angle rather than at 45° as it covers two horizontal canvas threads but only one vertical thread. It produces a smooth, flat surface on the canvas and is a very useful stitch to use as a contrast to more highly textured areas of stitching.

When you are choosing threads for working Gobelin stitches, make sure that your thread is thick enough to cover all the background canvas, without being so thick that it obscures the attractive texture.

HOW TO WORK GOBELIN STITCH

1 Take a stitch across two threads down-ward and one thread to the left, bringing the needle up again just to the right of the beginning of the first stitch.

2 Work a row of stitches in the same way across the area of canvas to be embroidered, by repeating step 1 the required number of times.

3 Work the next row by taking the needle from top to bottom, across two threads upward and one thread to the right. Repeat to the end of the row.

HOW TO WORK ENCROACHING GOBELIN STITCH

1 Take a stitch across five threads down-ward and one thread to the left, bringing the needle up again just to the right of the beginning of the first stitch.

2 Work a row of stitches in the same way across the area of canvas to be embroidered, by repeating step 1 the required number of times.

3 Bring the needle out four threads below the end stitch and work another row, inserting the needle so that the second row overlaps the first one by one thread.

HOW TO WORK PLAITED GOBELIN STITCH

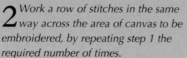  

1 Take a stitch across four threads upward and two threads to the right, bringing the needle out just to the right of the beginning of the first stitch.

2 Work a row of stitches in the same way across the area of canvas to be embroidered, by repeating step 1 the required number of times.

3 Work the second row of stitches slanting the opposite way, and overlapping the first row by one thread. Continue working rows in opposite directions.

Hungarian, Parisian, and brick stitches

Use these three variations on long stitch to add textures to your needlepoint; with careful planning, they can be made to imitate many different effects, from foliage to roof tiles.

Hungarian, Parisian, and brick stitches are variations on a theme; they are all composite stitches which use long, vertical stitches in different combinations and produce closely woven effects that can be built into your needlepoint projects to provide textural variety.

Although these stitches can be used in virtually any needlepoint design, their regular patterns make them ideal for pictorial scenes which include architectural details, such as houses and walls, and garden items such as shaped lawns, trees, and fences.

For instance, **Hungarian stitch** is formed by blocks of three stitches which form a rough hexagon or oval shape; this can be ideal for imitating foliage, floor tiles, roof tiles, patchwork quilts, etc., if you use different colors.

Brick stitch produces an interlocking pattern which can be used to echo its name if you work the stitches in red or brown or gray, or which could be worked in a straw color to give the effect of basketweave.

Parisian stitch produces blocks of stitching with even lines of texture across them; these are ideal worked in terracotta to imitate roof tiles, or stitched in varying shades of brown to produce a fence.

The stitches can all be varied in length, which makes them even more versatile. The overlapping stitches of brick stitch can be worked long, so that they suggest the bark lines of an old tree, or short so that they produce a tight, overlapping texture which could be used to give the impression of neat roof tiles. Although all three of the stitches are worked vertically, they can be turned on their side to produce horizontal lines of texture.

CHOOSING THREADS

When you work a diagonal stitch such as tent stitch, the threads of the background canvas are covered by the diagonal lie of the threads.

Because these three stitches are worked parallel with the threads of the canvas, you need to choose a thicker thread – or a smaller gauge of canvas – than normal, so that your stitches do not look gappy. Work a sample using your chosen thread and canvas, and see whether you are left with visible threads between the stitches; if so, adjust your materials slightly.

HOW TO WORK HUNGARIAN STITCH

1 *Begin by making a block of three vertical stitches. The first stitch goes over two threads of canvas, the middle one over four, and the third over two again.*

2 *Leaving a gap of one hole between the blocks, stitch the other blocks of three stitches in the same way and at the same level.*

3 *For the second row, stitch the blocks so that each long thread goes into the center hole between the two blocks in the row above.*

HOW TO WORK PARISIAN STITCH

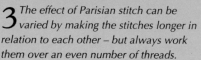

1 *Stitch the first row by making a continuous line of vertical stitches, alternately going over two and four threads of canvas.*

2 *For subsequent rows, work so that the long stitches of the next row slot into the notches made by the short stitches of the row above.*

3 *The effect of Parisian stitch can be varied by making the stitches longer in relation to each other – but always work them over an even number of threads.*

HOW TO WORK BRICK STITCH

1 *Begin with a row of stitches worked over two threads of canvas, but stagger each stitch in the row by working one stitch upward, then one downward.*

2 *Work all subsequent rows of brick stitch in the same way as shown in step 1 so that the stitches meet to form a regular interlocking pattern.*

3 *The effect achieved by brick stitch can be varied by making the stitches longer in relation to each other. This creates a more open effect.*

Long-legged cross-stitch

Cross-stitch has several variations, which are simple to work and give a textured appearance to needlepoint. Long-legged cross-stitch is one of these.

An interesting alternative to simple cross-stitch, long-legged cross-stitch can be worked equally successfully on single or double canvas, or on evenweave fabric. Its main distinguishing feature is that one "leg" of the cross is longer than the other, which produces a regular, plaited effect when the stitch is worked in rows.

TRADITIONAL USES

Long-legged cross-stitch has been used throughout the centuries and in many countries as part of their embroidery tradition. Some of its alternative names – plaited Slav stitch and Portuguese stitch – reflect this, while other names such as twist stitch or long-armed cross-stitch describe its appearance.

It was used instead of simple cross-stitch in early Assisi work, which originated in Italy. This is a form of embroidery in which the motifs are outlined in Holbein stitch (double running stitch) and left unfilled, while the background is filled in around them with one of the forms of cross-stitch. It was usually worked in red or blue with black outlines and often featured birds or animals and sometimes mythological motifs.

A variety of patterns which included long-legged cross-stitch were traditionally used by embroiderers in Eastern Europe. Their embroideries were often worked on bands of open-mesh scrim which were basted to the chosen background fabric, usually white cotton or linen. After the design had been worked, the scrim was cut in several places and the threads withdrawn from the work, leaving the embroidery against the plain white background fabric. The designs were often geometric, sometimes including stylized flowers, and the bands were used to decorate the front openings of peasant blouses and shirts.

A VERSATILE STITCH

Long-legged cross-stitch can be used in needlepoint to fill in large areas quite speedily, but it is also suitable for simple geometric designs and for decorative borders made up of bands of different colors. In needlepoint samplers, bands of long-legged cross-stitch could be used to separate different design elements.

As long-legged cross-stitch has a pronounced texture, the effect it produces varies according to the size of the stitches. If the stitch is worked small and in tight rows, it gives a densely woven effect, covering the canvas well. Larger stitches give a more loosely woven appearance.

Unlike simple cross-stitch, in which larger areas and borders can be worked in rows of half-stitches, with the stitch being completed on the return row, each stitch in basic long-legged cross-stitch is completed as you go along. Although the front of the work looks quite complex, the back consists simply of neat rows of vertical stitches.

HOW TO WORK LONG-LEGGED CROSS-STITCH

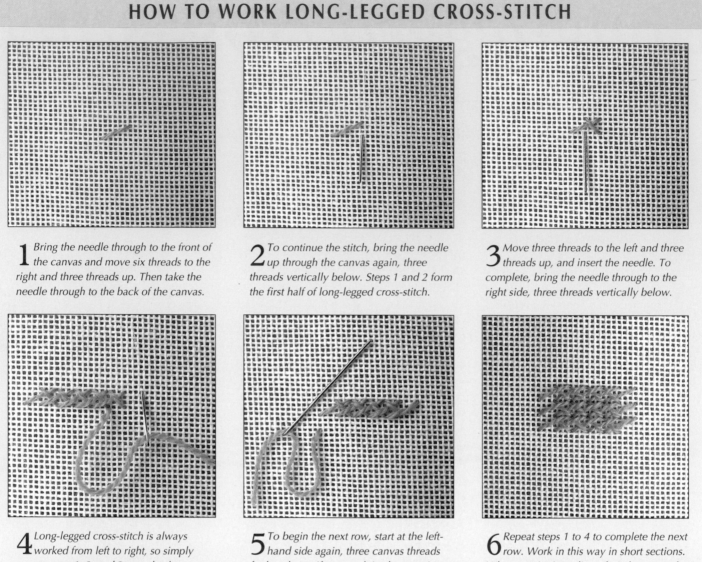

1 *Bring the needle through to the front of the canvas and move six threads to the right and three threads up. Then take the needle through to the back of the canvas.*

2 *To continue the stitch, bring the needle up through the canvas again, three threads vertically below. Steps 1 and 2 form the first half of long-legged cross-stitch.*

3 *Move three threads to the left and three threads up, and insert the needle. To complete, bring the needle through to the right side, three threads vertically below.*

4 *Long-legged cross-stitch is always worked from left to right, so simply repeat steps 1, 2, and 3 to make the next stitch and continue in this way to complete the row, ending with step 1.*

5 *To begin the next row, start at the left-hand side again, three canvas threads further down. If you work in short sections, you can thread the yarn through the back of the previous stitches.*

6 *Repeat steps 1 to 4 to complete the next row. Work in this way in short sections. When continuing a line of stitches, complete the last stitches of the previous rows for an unbroken "seam".*

VARIATIONS

For the top band, work every other cross-stitch, first leg only, from left to right. Then complete the short legs from right to left. Now fill in the missing stitches in the same way –first the long legs from left to right, then the short legs from right to left.

For the multicolored band, work as above, but change color for each leg.

For the bottom band, work all the long legs from left to right first. Then return right to left with the short legs to finish each stitch.

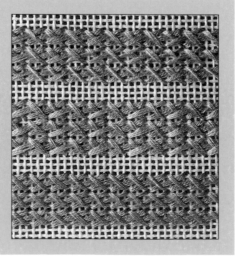

THE BACK VIEW

Basic long-legged cross-stitch looks much simpler on the back of the work than on the front. It consists of single vertical stitches spaced at regular intervals.

Smyrna stitch

Smyrna stitch is very simple to work, being a variation of basic cross-stitch. It will add variety and texture to your needlepoint and makes a useful border stitch.

Smyrna stitch is also known as Leviathan stitch, double cross-stitch, or railway stitch. It is an adaptation or an extension of simple cross-stitch, in that it is first worked diagonally in the usual way and then an upright cross is added over the top.

Although it is basically a needlepoint stitch, Smyrna stitch can also be used on evenweave fabric in combination with other cross-stitch variations. When working on canvas, it is important to choose the size of the canvas and the thickness of the thread very carefully, as it is sometimes difficult to cover the background threads completely. It may be necessary, for example, to reduce the size of the stitch or to use more strands of yarn. If more strands are used, it becomes easier to tease them apart slightly if necessary to cover any canvas threads which still show.

Keeping the tension of the stitches reasonably loose will also help to make sure that the canvas is covered well. If unsightly areas of canvas show between stitches or between rows, work lines of backstitches the same length or half the length of each Smyrna stitch between the rows to cover the gaps.

GEOMETRIC DESIGNS

Smyrna stitch is ideal for geometric designs, where it can be worked in different sizes or combined with other suitable stitches such as counted satin stitch or tent stitch. Bear in

mind that the same sequence should be followed when working each stitch. This is particularly important in geometric designs where a sudden change in direction would stand out as an obvious mistake.

When planning a design that includes both normal cross-stitch and Smyrna stitch, remember that Smyrna stitches are bulkier than cross-stitches; it may therefore be necessary to emphasize the cross-stitches in some way, perhaps by choosing a stronger-color yarn. Simply working the cross-stitches bigger is not enough, as this tends to give them a comparatively spindly look.

VARIATIONS

The look of Smyrna stitch can be varied by using two or more colors in combination. Work the first half of the stitch, i.e. the basic diagonal cross-stitch, in one color, with the second upright cross-stitch in a harmonizing or contrasting color. This can look very effective in a border design or as part of a block design in a sampler. Alternatively combine different colored strands of embroidery thread or Persian yarn in the needle. This gives a tweedy look, but tends to obliterate the texture of the stitch. The other obvious way of combining several colors is to complete each stitch in a single color, but bring in the variation by interchanging the colors in zigzag steps, diagonal lines, or checkerboard patterns.

HOW TO WORK SMYRNA STITCH

1 Bring the needle through to the front of the canvas and make a stitch diagonally up to the left over four threads, bringing it out four threads below.

2 Complete the first cross by making a stitch diagonally up to the right. Bring the needle out at the base of the stitch, halfway between the "legs" of the cross.

3 Take the needle four threads up to make a vertical stitch, bringing it out again at the left-hand side two canvas threads further down.

4 Finish the upright cross by working a horizontal stitch over four canvas threads. Bring the needle out at the bottom left to begin the next stitch.

YARN EFFECTS

Here, several rows of Smyrna stitch have been worked to show the textured pattern which is achieved by mixing shades of wool yarn.

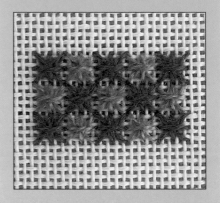

To vary the pattern made by rows of Smyrna stitch, alternate different shades of yarn to give a checkerboard effect as shown here.

WHAT WENT WRONG?

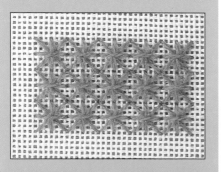

When Smyrna stitch is worked over too great a number of canvas threads, it makes a more open pattern and does not cover the canvas properly.

VARIATIONS

Smyrna stitch is ideal to use with tent stitch. The difference in the two stitches gives an interesting contrast.

This grid-like pattern is produced when the lower diagonal and upper straight crosses are worked in different colors.

HALF CROSS-STITCH

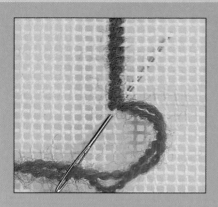

For a vertical row of stitches, bring the needle out and make the stitch in the hole diagonally below and left. Start the next stitch in the hole to the right of the thread.

A vertical row of half cross-stitch produces horizontal stitches on the back. Conversely, a horizontal row gives vertical stitches on the reverse of the work.

SPLIT STITCH

Split stitch is worked in a similar way to stem stitch, using a back and forth movement along the line to be covered. Split the thread with the point of the needle each time it emerges from the fabric. Keep the stitches small and even.

MOUNTING CANVAS

One way of mounting needlepoint over a piece of cardboard for a picture is to lace it across the back. Use strong thread and begin lacing from the center of one long side out toward the edge, securing the thread firmly.

Lace the thread from one side to the other in zigzag steps, taking a small stitch several canvas threads in from the edge at regular intervals. Pull the canvas taut as you go. Fasten the thread off securely.

Complete lacing the long side by working out from the center again to the other edge. Fold the corners under neatly on the short sides and then lace these together from top to bottom in the same way as for the long sides.

FRENCH KNOT

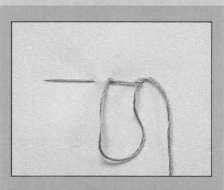

1 Hold point of needle close to point where thread emerges and, holding the thread taut with the left hand, wind thread round the needle two or three times.

HOW TO ATTACH CANVAS TO A SCROLL FRAME

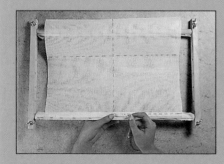

1 Mark the center of your canvas and the center of each length of rod tape. Place one edge over the tape on one rod and sew canvas and tape together with running stitch or backstitch using strong thread.

2 Sew canvas to tape on the other rod in the same way. Turn rods until canvas is taut and centred. Fix rods in position by tightening wing nuts and lace string (not shown) along unstretched edges of canvas on both sides.

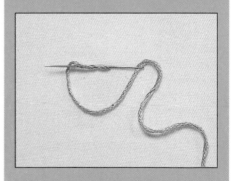

2 Holding thread in the left hand, tighten the twists and insert the needle in the fabric a few threads from where it emerged. Pull through to back of fabric to secure knot.

Mail-order kits

As an added benefit to our readers, we are able to offer a selection of the projects in this book as mail-order kits (see list below). All kits include plain canvas, needle, Paternayan Persian pure wool tapestry yarn, stitch chart and instructions.

For prices and availability, please contact:
Shillcraft Inc.
8899 Kelso Drive
Baltimore
MD 21221
Tel. (800) 566 3064

> Should you not require any of the offers listed below, you may still like a FREE copy of Shillcraft's craft catalog. Send your name and address to Shillcraft at the address on the left and Shillcraft will rush a copy to you by return.

ITEM	CODE	DESCRIPTION	PAGE
1	72591	Daffodil pillow kit	9
2	78468	Florentine pillow kit	17
3	77151	Star pillow kit	25
4	77057	Islamic pillow kit	29
5	78464	Fruit urn pillow kit	37
6	78339	Vine bolster kit	41
7	72312	Rose garden picture kit	45
8	77030	Cat door-stop kit	65
9	72501	Floral rug kit	73
10	72903	Noah's Ark picture kit	81

Index

A

Assisi work 121

B

bargello bench cushion 69–72
bargello pillow 17–21
basketweave
    brick stitch 119–20
    long stitch 61–64
basketweave tent stitch 113
beginners, projects 52, 82
bell pull 19
bias binding 107–8
blocking 103–4
bolster 41–44, 90–92
borders
    animals 21–24
    diamond 25–28
    oriental 29–32
    ribbon 41–44
    trellis 9–12
braids 109–10
brick stitch 25–28, 119–20

C

canvas
    blocking 103–4
    grain 113
    mounting 125
    types 111
cat door-stop 65–68, 96
cat picture 85–86
charts, marking 48
color
    combining 32
    long stitch 116
    matching décor 18
    shading 18, 43, 63
    Smyrna stitch 123–24
    substituting color combinations 18, 20, 28,
        32, 63, 72
continental tent stitch see tent stitch
cords
    attaching 15–16, 20, 28, 44
    making 109–10
cross-stitch 49–50, 73–76
    half 38, 43, 125
    long-legged 25–28, 121–22

D

daffodil pillow 9–12
dolphin pillow 21–24, 89
door-stop 65–68, 96
double cross-stitch 123
duck pillow 77–80

F

fabrics
    see also canvas
    damask 13–16
    needles 99–100
    pillow backing 40
    piping 16
    threads 101–2
    velvet 41–44
fan pillow 33–36
faults
    cords 110
    needles 100
    pillows 106
    Smyrna stitch 124
floral rug 73–76
Florentine needlepoint see bargello
flowers
    daffodils 9–12
    narcissi 9–12
    roses 33–36, 45–48, 70–73
    tulips 13–16
    violas 49–50
framing 36, 40, 54
French knots 22–24, 58, 125
fringing 76
fruit urn pillow 37–40

G

geometric mirror case 59–60
ginger cat picture 85–86
Gobelin stitches 22–24, 117–18
grapes 41–44

H

half cross-stitch, techniques 38, 43, 125
hall bench cushion 69–72
Hungarian stitch 119–20

I

Islamic pillow 29–32

L

Leviathan stitch 123
long stitch
    basketweave 61–64
    diamond shapes 14–15
    projects 22–24, 25–28, 55–59, 115–16
long-legged cross-stitch 25–28, 121–22

M

mirror case 59–60
mounting 125

N

narcissi 9–12
needles 99–100
Noah's Ark picture 81–84

O

oriental rugs, designs 30

P

Parisian stitch 119–20
patio garden picture 51–54
pen holder 87–88
petit point see tent stitch
pictures
    animals 24
    fans 36
    framing 36, 40, 54
    fruit urn 40
    ginger cat 85–86
    hanging 50
    Noah's Ark 81–84
    patio garden 51–54
    rose garden 45–48
    Spring 55, 94
    viola 49–50
pillows
    backing fabrics 40
    bargello 17–21
    daffodils 9–12
    dolphin 21–24, 89
    fans 33–36
    faults 106
    finishing 16, 20, 28, 40, 44, 105–6
    forms 105–6
    fruit urn 37–40
    Islamic 29–32

piping 16, 30, 107–8
potpourri 106
sheldduck 77–80
stars 25–28, 93
tulips 13–16
vine bolster 41–44, 90–92
piping 16, 30, 107–8
potpourri, pillows 106
pressing 104

R

railway stitch 123
rose garden picture 45–48
roses
    fan picture 33–36
    rug 73–76
rugs
    floral 73–76
    oriental designs 30

S

scroll frames 125
seat cover 69–72
sheldduck pillow 77–80
Smyrna stitch 61–64, 123–24
split stitch 65–68, 125
spring picture 55–58, 94
star pillow 25–28, 93
stretching 103–4
swatch cards 10, 42

T

tapestry 117
tent stitch
    basketweave 113–14
    continental 111–12
    projects 25–28, 59–60, 65–68, 77–80
threads 101–2
    braids 109–10

combining colors 84
cords 109–10
needles 99–100
preparing to stitch 43
specifications 8
starting and finishing 10–12, 30, 40, 48
swatch cards 10, 42
tension 43, 44
tissue box cover 61–64, 95
tulip pillow 13–16

V

vine bolster 41–44, 90–92
viola picture 49–50

Y

yarns *see* threads

Index compiled by INDEXING SPECIALISTS, *Hove*